BEST OF THE
★★★★★
BLACK POT

MUST-HAVE
DUTCH OVEN
FAVORITES

MARK'S BLACK POT

BEST ⋆⋆⋆⋆ OF THE BLACK POT

MUST-HAVE DUTCH OVEN FAVORITES

MARK HANSEN

HOBBLE CREEK PRESS
AN IMPRINT OF CEDAR FORT, INC.
SPRINGVILLE, UTAH

ISBN 13: 978-1-59955-971-1

Published by Hobble Creek Press, an imprint of Cedar Fort, Inc.
2373 W. 700 S., Springville, UT 84663
Distributed by Cedar Fort, Inc., www.cedarfort.com

LIBRARY OF CONGRESS CATALOGING-IN-PUBLICATION DATA

Hansen, Mark (Rulon Mark), author.
  The best of the black pot : must-have Dutch oven favorites / Mark Hansen.
    pages cm
  ISBN 978-1-59955-971-1
  1. Dutch oven cooking. 2. Cooking, American. I. Title.

  TX840.D88H36 2012
  641.5'89--dc23

                        2011050113

Cover design by Angela D. Olsen
Cover design © 2012 by Lyle Mortimer
Edited and typeset by Kelley Konzak

Printed in the United States of America

10 9 8 7 6 5 4 3 2 1

Printed on acid-free paper

PRAISE FOR
BEST OF THE BLACK POT

"Mark Hansen makes Dutch oven cooking sound and feel like fun! Anyone picking up this book will be heading out to buy their first Dutch oven. It's very informative, with easy-to-follow recipes, and a little history of each. I would recommend this cookbook to all beginners and also to the more 'seasoned' Dutch oven cooks."

—Omar Alvarez, Winner of the 2008 IDOS
World Championship Dutch Oven Cook-off

"I'd call it 'Everything you ever wanted to know about dutch oven cooking . . . and then some.' Dutch oven cooking can be intimidating to the beginner, but this book is full of easy-to-understand information. There is something for both the novice and seasoned black pot chef. This book is full of good recipes, fun stories, and insights on life. Reading it feels like a conversation with an old friend."

—Toni Black, dutchovenmadness.blogspot.com

"Mark has gone the extra mile and made this book self-explanatory. Beginners will be thrilled with the simple, easy way he explains the cooking directions. Every cook starts somewhere, and this book comes highly recommended from me!"

—Colleen Sloan, author of the Log Cabin Grub series

"Mark has written a fantastic book full of black pot magic. This book is a must-have for the Dutch oven enthusiast, whether beginner or pro."

—Matt Pelton, author of *The Cast Iron Chef*
and *From Mountaintop to Tabletop*

CONTENTS

INTRODUCTION

SOME RANDOM THOUGHTS TO GET US STARTED

MY STORY

IT'S FUNNY to me to think that I'm writing a cookbook. I'm not a professional chef with a restaurant. I don't have a culinary degree. Up until just a few years ago, I had very little interest in cooking at all. So, how did I get from apathy to author? From blasé to baker? Would you mind if I retraced my steps?

My mom was an excellent cook, and in a lot of ways, she shaped how I approach cooking, even though I had very little interest in it as I was growing up. She cooked most things from scratch, and she was always trying new things from cuisines all over the world. While other kids had Wonder bread peanut butter sandwiches, I was raised on her whole wheat bread and her carob chip cookies.

True, a few things she made I hated as a child. There's no surprises there. All kids hate certain things until they grow up. Still, her willingness to risk new recipes and new ideas and her enthusiasm for making things from scratch are things that I've discovered in my own cooking now.

My sister took to the kitchen with gusto, learning many American, ethnic, and exotic dishes. Her abilities got her jobs in restaurant kitchens. Years later, she married a man who had also been a chef.

All that time, however, I just wasn't that interested.

In my early adulthood, I was able to cook to survive, but not much else. I had a repertoire of about a dozen or so dishes that I could cook over and over. I did a chicken and hot sauce dish that I rather liked. I could grill a hamburger about as well as anyone else I knew. There was this onion soup that I had picked up while in Central America. I could add a few others that I can't think of right now onto that list, but it's still a short one.

1

My wife did more cooking than I did, and that was fine with me. She was always good at it.

Then, in June of 2006, she surprised me with a Father's Day present. She had remembered somewhere back in her mind that I had at some time mentioned that I had thought that maybe it might be kinda cool to figure out how to maybe learn a little bit about cooking in a Dutch oven. Kinda. Sorta. You know . . .

The present was a 12-inch, shallow Lodge Dutch oven. To this day, it's still one of my favorites. I was very excited. I had thought, apparently, that it would be great to learn how to cook for our family camping trips that happened once or twice every summer. I surmised that if I was to do that, I had better get a little practice in first.

I read the instructions and seasoned the oven. I did some research online and looked over recipes. I decided that the first thing I would cook would be pizza.

I think it was beginner's luck, but the pizza was a big hit with the family, and it grew from there. Pretty soon, I was cooking all of our Sunday dinners in my new Dutch oven. I got books, I hit the Net, I researched recipes. I had flops and hits. To this day, for example, I feel sorry for my family members that had to choke down my first attempt at apple pie.

Then, early in 2007, a good friend of mine, John, came in to work and mentioned that he'd been thinking about starting another blog. I say "another blog" because we had both been experimenting with this (then) relatively new phenomenon for a while at that point. We both had a couple of blogs we were running. My first reaction was, "Why on earth do you need another blog?"

He laughed because he knew he didn't have a good answer for that, but he set it up anyway. He called it "Confessions of a Mormon Foodie," and he put it at mormon foodie.com. Over the course of the next few months, he and I talked a lot about food and cooking. I learned a lot from him in just that short period.

The big part is that he got me enthused for food blogging. Soon I had decided that I would jump in as well. I could blog my Dutch oven recipes and stories, and the path of my learning.

I learned soups, stews, and roasts. I learned how to buy and use a knife. I learned how to make pasta from scratch and to roll it by hand. I learned how to knead and bake artisan breads. I learned from John, from my sister, from my mom, and from Jodi. I learned from YouTube, *Good Eats*, and *America's Test Kitchen*.

All along the way, I shared what I was learning. *Mark's Black Pot* grew, entry by entry, click by click. I wasn't an expert back then, and really, I'm still not. I'm just sharing what I'm learning.

Thanks for coming along for the ride.

WHY I DUTCH OVEN

I've been enjoying Dutch oven cooking for a few years now, and I've noticed some things about myself. At times, as I've sat on my back porch, watching the coals burn down on top of an oven, I've wondered why I do it and why I enjoy it so much. Here are some of the reasons . . .

I DO IT TO UNPLUG

My life is tech-driven. I make my living on the phone and on the Net. I come home, and I spend more time on the Net. I carry my cell phone with me at all times. My cell is also my tunes and my day planner. When I play card games with my kids, I use my cell to keep score. I relax in front of a good *Law and Order* episode on my satellite TV. I'm a blogger. What more do I need to say?

However, when I cook Dutch, I'm unplugged. There are no wires, no connections. It's just me, the food, the pots, the coals. I don't even have to be "in the wild." I can be sitting on my back porch, and I'm still suddenly off the grid.

I DO IT TO UNWIND

When I'm cooking our family's Sunday dinner, there's no pressure. I don't have to get anything cooked by a specific time, and there's no worries if it's the greatest dish of all time.

Now, there are times when I'm having company over or it's a holiday dinner, and it gets a little crazy. I want those meals to be amazing. There are those times when I cook publicly or at a cook-off. At those times, I feel more pressure. But most of the time, it's a time for me to unwind. Most of the time, I get the chance to think, to wait.

I don't choose my recipes because they're quick. There're no cast-iron microwaves. Sometimes I choose my recipes deliberately because I know they're going to take more than an hour to prepare and two more to cook.

Don't bother me. I'm cooking.

I DO IT TO EXPERIMENT

And while I'm talking about recipes, I don't choose them because they're simple, either. One thing I love about Dutching is that you can cook almost anything in it. So I want to push that envelope and see what I can do, what I can learn. Finding a new recipe is part of the challenge. I love it when I do something and people are surprised that it can be done in a Dutch oven.

I DO IT TO CONNECT TO THE PAST

There's a small part of me that, from time to time, thinks back to my Mormon pioneer ancestors, driven from their homes in beautiful Nauvoo and following their faith across the open yet hostile plains. I think about them stopping on the way and pulling out their Dutch ovens and cooking the evening's meal.

I know I don't suffer like they did. Even still, sometimes I think about it.

I DO IT TO CONNECT WITH FRIENDS

Cooking for other people is cool. I love it when I can pull off one of my favorite dishes and see them dive in, then sit back, full and happy.

Cooking with other people is cool too. Even at competitions, there is friendship, camaraderie, and a desire to help each other out. And after the judging is done and we're all waiting for the prize announcements, we all share our feasts with each other. That's the best part.

It's also fun to plug back in and hang with my new friends on the Net, most of whom I've never met face-to-face. But I've tried some of their recipes and read their advice, and I feel like some of them are my Dutchin' mentors.

I DO IT TO PREPARE

With all this emotion and philosophy, there's also a practical side. I know that if there were a power outage or some other kind of emergency issue, my family would not only be able to eat, but they would also eat well.

And last of all, at the end of the day, we get to sit down to dinner. And most of the time, it tastes *great!*

That feels good.

THOUGHTS ON "THE RIGHT WAY TO DO IT"

I've encountered an interesting phenomenon in the cooking world. It's called "the right way."

I began to discover it about the same time that I started taking my knife skills seriously. I figured that since the Internet is a priceless and vast source of all learning and wisdom, I could surely learn how to hold and use a chef's knife. Right? Just Google it!

I went straight to YouTube. There, I found a vast pantry full of videos about choosing, sharpening, holding, and wielding chef's knives. I think I watched every one of them. There were many different ways shown to dice, slice, and chop. Each chef demonstrating the technique told me that his or her way was "the right way" and that all of the others were crazy because they were showing me "the wrong way."

I noticed this phenomenon cropping up all over. Every time I looked up a new recipe or a new cooking technique, someone tried to tell me that it needed to be done "the right way."

At first, I was confused. But gradually, after watching so many videos, I came away with an idea of how to do certain cuts, how to hold my knife, how not to chop off my fingers with the carrots, and so on. I learned how to do it. It might not be "the right way," but it's been workin' so far!

Even in the Dutch oven world, there are "right way-ers." Many think that they know the "right way" to season a Dutch oven, or to place their coals, or to clean it out afterward. The debates rage. Detergent? Aluminum foil? Don't get us started!

I finally arrived at this point: People have been cooking food for millennia. They've been cooking it in cast iron for centuries. There's probably more than one way to do everything.

Let's get real, here. I don't really know what I'm doing. However, I've learned some cool techniques. I'm still sorting out some of them, and others have become "my way." I've written the recipes in this book to show "my way." I hope I never try to force anyone to believe that means they're always "the right way."

BACKYARD COOKING

Many people associate the Dutch oven with camping. Rightly so. My proud pioneer ancestors that crossed the western plains used it as they camped each night on the way. Lewis and Clark used it as they camped along their journey. Modern campers are discovering just how tasty and fancy they can get while out in the great outdoors.

Me? Not so much.

While I, at times, do enjoy camping, and I *love* to cook in the open air or by a bubbling stream, I don't get out into the wilderness very often. I might go camping once, maybe twice a year.

But as my good friend Andy (backporchgourmet.com) reminds us after every blog post, "The Outdoors Start at Your Back Porch." I've really taken that to heart. I love cooking in my Dutch oven, right on my back porch (or my front porch, if it's raining). Many Dutch oveners over the years have commented to me that they're amazed that I cook in my Dutch ovens so often, but I'm not alone. Toni at dutch ovenmadness.com set out to cook her family dinners in hers every night for a year. And she's still going at it!

My point is that you don't need to wait for that camping trip, that big family gathering, or that Dutch oven gathering or cook-off to try it. Just have a nice, relaxing

Sunday afternoon, watching the coals burn down on a roasting chicken and some biscuits. Mmmmmm . . .

"MESSING WITH THE RECIPE"

Okay, one last bit of fluffy philosophizing, and then we'll get to the cooking.

Several months ago, as I was contemplating cooking and my other hobby, music, my dear wife suggested I combine them and write a song about cooking. I got to thinking about that, and I came up with the tune below. It kinda summarizes my approach to cooking and my approach to life as well.

As I've been learning to cook, I've encountered a lot of people, most of whom fall into one of two categories. Those that follow recipes with unquestioning, meticulous accuracy, and those who just "wing it." Fortunately, there are a lot of shades in between as well, and that's where I seem to fall.

MESSIN' WITH THE RECIPE
by Mark Hansen, with Jodi Hansen

19 February 2011

Some people I know
When they cook
Double-check the recipe
And follow the book
They measure every spice
They sift and pour
Doing to perfection
What's been done before
No reason to question
No reason to doubt
Somebody else already
Figured it out
So why go
Messin' with the recipe?

Some people I know
When they're in the kitchen
Work fast and free
With their imagination
A little of this and
A pinch of that
What should we add
Well, what've we got?
No time to wonder
No time to waste

Just throw it in
And see how it'll taste
So why bother
Messin' with a recipe?

Is it savory or is it sweet?
Is it dessert or is it meat?
Do you like the smell?
Do you like the flavor?
Do you chomp it down
Or is it a dish to savor?

Now I'm not a chef
But when I'm cooking
I'll have the book open
And I'm always looking
But I can't ever leave
Well enough alone
I'm dashing, splashing flavors
Stirring all on my own
Sometimes I hit
Sometimes I botch
But I always try
To kick it up a notch
Seems I'm always
Messin' with the recipe

Is your life savory or is it sweet?
Is your life dessert or is it meat?
Do you like the smell?
Do you like the flavor?
Do you chomp it down
Or is it a dish to savor?
Seems I'm always
Messin' with the recipe

The tune can be heard at http://www.marksblackpot.com/p/song.html.

HOW TO USE THIS BOOK

This book is a little different than many cookbooks, I hope. I've tried to set it up so that it's much like my blog. The recipes are more like stories than straight instructions. I hope that makes them a little more fun to read. Every once in a while, as it seems relevant, I've added some pages of hints, instructions, or thoughts—not strictly recipes, but I hope they prove helpful. Finally, at the end of each chapter, I've added some additional recipes from our family collection. I've edited them and altered them for Dutch oven use, but they're not necessarily "Dutch oven" recipes, and they haven't appeared on the blog. They're just bonuses for the book!

If you're a follower of marksblackpot.com, I thank you very much for all the fun. I'm grateful to you for reading, for posting comments, and for trying the recipes.

If you got this book some other way, I invite you to check out the blog and post some comments as you're inspired. Send me your recipes, and I'll try them out. Tell me your Dutch oven stories, and I'll share them too! We'll cook together!

CHAPTER 1

EASY DUTCH OVEN COOKING

COOKING CAN be as complex or as simple as you want it to be. The best way to approach it is to start with the simple stuff and work your way up to the more complex things. Still, along the way, I don't think "simple" or "easy" should mean "bland" or "lame." I always try to make everything I do as tasty and flavorful as possible!

DUTCH OVEN HEAT

First of all, as we get started, here are some thoughts on heat:

It was an interesting revelation when it hit me that cooking is fundamentally simple. I mean, we've been doing it for thousands and thousands of years. There are lots of ways to do it, and we can cook in different kinds of ovens, stoves, hearths, grills, and griddles. Still, the bottom line with all of these varying methods is: You're applying heat to food.

That's all it is.

How you do that and how much of it you do has varied over the centuries and from one continent to another. Cultures and civilizations rise and fall. Through it all, cooking is all about one thing:

Applying heat to food.

Now, in the Dutch oven world, you do it by putting something smoldering under and/or on top of the Dutch oven. That can be wood burned down to coals or it can be commercially made charcoal briquettes. For my backyard kitchen, I use briquettes, because they're easy to control and easy to light. If you use the good brands, they'll burn long and steady. The cheap ones give off inconsistent heat and burn out too fast. You don't need fancy mesquite or smoke flavoring because none of that smoke will get through the cast iron to the food anyway.

In most Dutch oven recipes, you need heat coming up from the bottom and heat coming down from the top. The "camp" Dutch ovens have a lip around the lid that keeps the coals on top and the ash out of your food.

As a general rule, It's said that two briquettes, one above and one below, will produce about 20–25 degrees of heat. I'm not sure if the measurement is really that linear. I suspect that the higher in temperature you go, the greater the proportion of coals you have to add on. I don't have any data to back this up yet, however. Someday, I'd love to spend the whole day just putting coals on various sizes of Dutch ovens and measuring the internal heat. Just to see . . .

Someday.

In the meantime, I've worked out this chart, partly from other charts that I've pulled from all over, and mostly from my own experience:

DO size	300°	325°	350°	375°	400°	425°	450°	475°
8″	12–14	13–16	15–18	17–19	18–20	19–21	20–23	21–24
10″	16–18	18–21	20–23	23–25	24–26	25–28	27–30	28–32
12″	19–22	22–25	25–28	27–29	28–32	30–33	33–36	36–40
14″	24–28	27–31	30–33	32–35	35–38	38–41	40–43	43–47

This chart is for basic baking and almost all of the cooking that I do. Compare the size of the Dutch oven to the desired temperature and you'll get an approximate amount of total coals to use. This is a range because there are many variables that can impact the final temperature. If it's a hot day or you're using a "shallow" Dutch oven, go lower. If it's a cold day, it's a windy day, or you're using a "deep" Dutch oven, go higher. If you're not sure, go in the middle. Cooking is actually pretty forgiving.

If you're baking or doing most one-pot meals, put about a third of the coals below and about two thirds of them above, on the lid. If you're boiling or simmering, put either all the coals on the bottom or a third above and two-thirds below. If you're roasting, then split the total number of coals evenly between the top and bottom.

The recipes in this book list how many coals to put where. Truly, the best way to learn heat management is by experience. Just try it! I hold my hand over the ovens about a foot or so in the air to learn how hot that feels. I can tell how the weather conditions of the day are changing the temperature of the oven. That comes with practice.

There's another simple method of setting out the coals that's gaining a lot of popularity. Rather than counting out the coals, you simply create rings of coals. Form a circle with your coals so that each coal is close to its neighbor, even touching. A half ring would be missing every other coal.

This system is much simpler, breaking the cooking process down into four basic heat measurements: Slow (about 300°), Medium (350°), Hot (400°), and Very Hot (450°). In most cases, I've found that you don't need to be any more precise than that, even in baking.

Dutch Oven Size	Slow	Medium	Hot	Very Hot
8″	½ ring	¾ ring	1¼ rings	1½ rings
10″	¾ ring	1 ring	1½ rings	2 rings
12″	1 ring	1½ rings	2 rings	2½ rings
14″	1½ rings	2 rings	2½ rings	3 rings
16″	2 rings	2½ rings	3 rings	3½ rings

The rings in the chart are the amounts for the coals you put above the lid. In all cases, put one ring on the bottom. In long cook times, as coals burn down, move them together, and fill in the empty spaces with new coals.

Personally, I'm not married to either method. The ring method is convenient, and I suspect it's more accurate. Not only are you using more rings to get hotter temperatures out of bigger Dutch ovens, but the fact that the ovens are larger will also mean that there are more coals in the rings. I think that might well take into account the heating curve I was talking about earlier.

The ring method doesn't take into account the various cooking methods (roasting, baking, simmering, sautéing, and so on), but with a bit of practice, you can adapt it.

When dealing with these measurements and charts, no matter which method you use, keep in mind that these are *not* sharp rules. The Dutch oven police won't come and arrest you if you miscount or if you have too many or too few. If you stray too far from these guidelines, then you might not get the results you wish.

If it's a windy day, a hot day, or a cold day (I like to Dutch oven even in the winter), these numbers will change. Cold weather requires more briquettes, sometimes up to 25 percent more. Windy days get more air to the coals, so there's more heat, but the coals burn faster.

It's also good to be careful how you place the coals. In most cases, You want to focus the heat on the rim of the oven. Set the bottom coals in a ring around the bottom edge of the oven. You want the coals fully under the oven, but not so much in the middle. This makes the heat travel down and up the sides of the oven and radiate toward the center. The same on top, as much as possible. Coals in the middle tend to create hotspots, which will burn the food. That's sometimes less critical on the lid, where it's not directly touching the food, usually. The picture above shows good coal placement for baking.

It's also important to keep a side fire going. Charcoals burn down, and if you're doing a recipe that takes longer than an hour or so to cook, you'll need more coals to add back to your ovens. When I start the coals to begin cooking, I always light what I think will be too many. The extras become my side fire. About a half hour into the cooking, I'll add another ten or so coals to that pile. The older coals will catch the new coals, and by the time I need more coals, I'll have them ready. I've ruined too many dishes (and at least one pie), by having my coals go out halfway through. By rotating my coals through a side fire, I can cook almost indefinitely.

It's good to have some long-handled tongs to grab and place the coals. Don't use your hands. It will hurt. Duh. It's also good to get some long-handled pliers or an actual "lid lifter" to check on the food.

For simmering, you've got liquid on the bottom that's going to disperse the heat anyway, so I just pack the coals in any way I can get them under the oven. Leave some space between the coals for ventilation, and a gap in the center.

When I roast, I still try to keep a bit clear of the center, but there are more coals to put down there, so you need to pack them in more. A second ring works, and some people go with a sort of checkerboard pattern.

Remember, all you're doing is applying heat to food. Do it a few times and you'll get better and better at it.

I've had a lot of people tell me various tricks they do, some of them elaborate, to keep the food from burning. They put platforms of cardboard wrapped in aluminum foil in the bottom or various other things to separate the heat from direct contact with the food. These things might work, but if you just practice and are careful, you'll soon learn that with careful management of the heat, you won't have to use these tricks and your food will turn out great. When in doubt, a little less heat is better than a little more. It might take a little longer to cook, but it's less likely to burn. Some foods are more forgiving than others too. It's tough to ruin a stew, but a bread or a cake is a bit more critical.

CHICKEN, POTATOES, AND ONIONS

A GREAT PLACE TO START

I hang out on a lot of groups on the Internet. It's an annoying habit, but I'm a Net junkie, and admitting it is the first step to recovery, right?

Anyway, once in one of the forums I'm on, we drifted off topic. One of the moms and I got into a side thread on Dutch ovening. She said that she was new to it and asked if I had any tips and recipes. Well, of course I have both!

DUTCH OVEN HERBAL CHICKEN WITH POTATOES AND ONIONS

Here's a recipe for a full meal dish that's pretty easy. I've done it a few times, and it's popular with the family. This one is also pretty cool, because if someone were to do this recipe right, they'd learn a lot of the basic techniques of Dutching, like heat management, rotating, and one-pot meals.

As you'll see, it's also flexible and adaptable. I cook this one frequently, and I've tried several variations.

TOOLS
10- or 12-inch Dutch oven
For the baking part: About 25 briquettes for a 12-inch oven,
    6–8 briquettes below, the rest above.

INGREDIENTS
1 pkg. bacon, cut into short pieces
3–5 medium to large potatoes, quartered and sliced
1–2 medium to large onions, sliced
1–2 green peppers, sliced
2–3 stalks of celery, sliced
3 chicken breasts, cut into small chunks
salt, seasoned salt, and pepper to taste
salsa, if you like that sorta thing. You could serve it plain and offer the salsa to be added
    on the plate after serving.

FLAVORINGS (HERBAL—STYLE)
1 heaping Tbsp. minced garlic
Liberal shakes of parsley, rosemary, oregano
A few shakes (about a tsp. or so) balsamic vinegar
And, of course, salt and pepper

I START by making sure that the chicken is good and thawed. I spread the breasts out on paper towels, blot them dry, then cut them into cubes of 1 inch or so. You can really cut them up any way you want. Then I slice and cut up all the ingredients. I find I can do that while the coals are preparing, but you can also do it beforehand.

I'll light some coals, and when they show some good white around the edges, I put about 15 or so under a seasoned 12-inch Dutch oven. As I mentioned before, I'll have about a half-dozen or so more lit coals off to the side. These will be my "side fire" and will help keep the coals fresh as they burn out. After the oven has heated up for a few minutes, I add the bacon, cut into short pieces and separated. I cook the bacon, stirring occasionally. I like it fairly crispy.

After about 15 or 20 minutes, when the bacon is about done, I'll want to add some fresh charcoal briquettes to the half dozen that are burning off to the side. They will light the new ones, and then I'll be able to use them to replenish the cooking coals.

When the bacon is how I like it, I take the oven off the coals temporarily. I add everything else in the ingredients list to the oven. I stir it all up to mix it and coat everything with the bacon flavor. I add the salt, pepper, and any other spices I like. You could do Cajun seasoning, hot sauce, poultry seasoning—whatever you like and have. There are some suggestions below. Don't be timid with the seasonings!

In the cooking area, I arrange about 7–8 hot coals in a circle about the size of the bottom of the oven. Then I place the oven on top of them. The coals should be fully under the oven, and right at the edge. I take the rest of the hot coals and some of the freshly lit ones (about 15–18 total) and place them on top, in a circle around the edge of the oven's lid. You can place a few of them in the center of the lid. I mark the time as the start of the cooking.

The total cooking time will probably be about 35–45 minutes, but your mileage may vary. I cook it until the potatoes are soft and the chicken is cooked through. About every 15–20 minutes, I lift the lid and check it, giving it a stir. When I replace the lid, I rotate it about a quarter turn. Then I lift the entire oven and rotate it about another quarter turn. This makes the briquettes close to different spots on the oven, and it lessens hot spots and burning.

As the briquettes burn, you might have to pull more briquettes from your side fire to replenish the ones on or below the oven. That's what they're there for! When I'm handling briquettes, I use long, spring-handled cooking tongs.

When it's done, I pull the oven aside and take off the coals. I tip the lid over the cooking space to shake the coals off the lid. Finally, I replace the lid on the Dutch oven. The oven and lid will retain the heat for quite some time (that's one of the cool things about cast iron).

When it's all done, I serve it right from the oven. After everyone's had seconds, I clean it with a plastic bristled brush and hot water, no soap. When it's all scrubbed clean and still warm from the water, I coat it with another very thin layer of oil or shortening (inside and out, lid as well). Over time, it'll build up more and more coating and become the best nonstick cookware you own.

This one's a really simple recipe, with few steps, but it really impresses people, and it's delicious! It's also easy to get creative with it and tweak the ingredients. It's very forgiving in the timing and the measuring.

VARIATIONS

Now, there are some really cool ways you can change this one up. Chicken, in many ways, is like an artist's canvas. You can really paint a lot of different flavors on top of it, and it will taste just great. These variations simply replace the flavorings section of the ingredients listed above. Other than that, the process is all pretty much the same.

SOME LIKE IT HOT

1 heaping Tbsp. minced garlic
1–2 jalapenos, sliced. If you don't like it really hot, you can seed and core them first or use less
a few shakes of cayenne pepper, chili powder, or Louisiana-style hot sauce (Tabasco)
a few shakes of paprika
about ½ bundle of fresh, chopped cilantro
juice of 1–2 limes
and, of course, salt and pepper

SPRINGTIME LEMON

1 heaping Tbsp. minced garlic
½ cup fresh chopped parsley
zest of 1 lemon
juice of 1–2 lemons
and, of course, salt and pepper

OTHER VARIATIONS

And here are a few more suggestions that will take this dish even further:

Pre-sauté the veggies. Cook the bacon in the Dutch oven over 15–20 coals, then remove most of the grease. Sauté the onions and garlic in the bacon grease until they're translucent and sweet. You might even add any celery or peppers to sauté as well. This will caramelize the veggies (especially the onions) and bring out the sugars. Then add the remaining ingredients and cook it all just the same as in the other methods.

Also, after you take the Dutch oven off the coals, but a few minutes before serving, coat the food with a layer of the appropriate kind of shredded cheese. Replace the lid and let the Dutch oven's residual heat melt it. For the herbal flavorings, I'd choose a mozzarella. For the hot version, I'd suggest a cheddar or Colby Jack. With the lemon style, I'd crumble up a handful of feta onto the plate as it's being served.

DUTCH OVEN APPLE AND ORANGE CHICKEN

Our church is very interested in the real-life, everyday well-being of people. One of the things they do for people is help with food in times of difficulty. In addition, one of the things that they do as you start to get food assistance is give you a recipe book. It's full of really good, basic recipes of dishes you can make with a few staple ingredients. It's got a lot of good advice on simple cooking skills. For example, if you're used to just pulling out the boxed biscuit mix to make biscuits, then you can use this recipe book to mix up your own. In other words, they don't just give you food; they also hope that you'll learn a bit more about how to cook it so you're better prepared to take care of your family.

Anyway, I was flipping through this recipe book, and there's some really cool stuff in it. I came across this recipe for apple and orange pork chops. Well, it turns out that we didn't have any pork chops, but we did have chicken, so I redid it. I can never leave a recipe alone, of course, so there are some extra herbs and spices in it too.

TOOLS
18–20 coals below, to start, then 8–9 coals below
16–18 coals above, to bake

INGREDIENTS
about 1 lb. boneless chicken, cubed
1 onion, sliced
2 cloves garlic, minced (about 1–2 Tbsp.)
salt and pepper
olive oil
1 cup uncooked rice
2 cups water
1 large apple, peeled and diced
2 oranges, peeled, separated, and diced
zest of 1 orange

FLAVORINGS
Your choice of herbs and spices. I used:
cinnamon
rosemary
oregano
thyme
and any additional salt or pepper that it might need.

THIS IS actually an easy dish to make. It's done in two steps.

First, I thawed the chicken and lit up the coals. I like to have it fully thawed and even patted dry so that the chicken doesn't add as much moisture to the overall dish. It'll also be easier to brown. I sometimes think it's a little easier to slice and dice chicken when it's still partly frozen, but in this case, I don't want the extra moisture.

Then I put the chicken, onion, and garlic in the open pot on the coals and let that start to brown. It took a little while. I recommend using more coals rather than fewer.

Then, as it was browning, it was time to work on the other ingredients. I zested, then peeled the oranges. I separated them and diced them. I peeled the apples, then sliced and diced them up.

Soon, the chicken and onions were ready. The onions were translucent and getting a brown edge, and the chicken was cooked and brown. I put in the rice, water, and fruit, and stirred it all up. I pulled some coals from the bottom to put on top and added more coals on top. I also had a side fire going to keep fresh coals for replenishing. From this point on, I was cautious about opening up the lid. If you let too much moisture escape, then the rice doesn't cook as well.

Then I went inside and chose some herbs and spices. In retrospect, I think it would be fun to use a different set. I might go for the more "sweet spices," like nutmeg with the cinnamon. And maybe just a touch of cayenne for some edge. Still, the ones I used tasted great.

About 45 minutes later, it was done.

Family and friends said it had a really cool Chinese taste. I think that was because of the oranges. It was both sweet and savory.

HOW TO BUY A DUTCH OVEN

I got a post on my Facebook fan page from someone asking about how to choose and buy a Dutch oven. Rather than reply there with what will be way too long of an answer for Facebook, I posted this article:

The simple answer is . . . Send me some money and I'll buy you one! :-)

I guess the real title for this article should be, "How to Shop for a Dutch Oven and Buy One That's the Best for You." There's a lot of "That depends on what you're looking for" in the answer, so let's break it down. I'm presuming, by the way, that those reading this are primarily interested in buying their first Dutch oven. If you've already got one or two and you're looking to buy another, you'll still be looking for the same basic things, but your reasons for buying will be different and you'll have a different result, possibly.

There are four basic variables that you'll want to consider when you're deciding which kind to buy: the type, the size, the material, and the quality.

THE TYPE

You have two basic options here: "camp" Dutch ovens or "stove" Dutch ovens. Which you choose will depend on what you're going to do with it.

A "camp" Dutch oven is primarily designed for outdoor cooking using wood coals or charcoal briquettes. It's got a lip around the perimeter of the lid that keeps the coals on the lid and prevents ash from falling down into the food when you lift it. It's also got legs on the bottom that lift the Dutch oven up above any coals you want to put underneath.

A "stove" Dutch oven is designed primarily for use indoors, in a conventional oven or on your stovetop. It won't have the legs, because you're setting it in your oven or resting it directly on your stove's burner. It doesn't have the lip around the lid because there's no coals to be put on top. Some of these will even be coated in colored enamels.

It *is* possible to use a camp Dutch oven indoors, but it's not as convenient. It's possible to use a stove Dutch oven outdoors, but it's tricky.

THE SIZE

Dutch ovens are primarily measured by diameter, and sometimes by quart capacity. Common sizes are 10- and 12-inch. You can buy them as small as 5-inch or as large as 22-inch (which take considerable effort to lift, even without food in them). Which one you end up buying will depend largely on who you'll be cooking for. If you're cooking for yourself or you have a small family, you won't want a big one. If you have a larger family or if you're thinking you'll end up cooking for groups of friends, you'll want a bigger one.

If this is your first oven and you're just interested in experimenting a little, I'd recommend a 12-inch, shallow oven. This will have the capacity to feed a family of four with some leftovers and can easily cook for a gathering of as many as eight, depending on what you're cooking. Breads, stews, chilis, desserts, and even small roasts can easily be done in a 12-inch Dutch oven.

Larger and smaller ovens will come in handy in more specialized situations. For example, I use my 14-inch ovens to cook turkeys and larger specialty meats. I use my 8-inch Dutch oven for sides of rice or sauces.

THE MATERIAL

There are two basic materials used to make Dutch ovens: cast iron and aluminum. There are advantages and disadvantages to both. Even though all of my Dutch ovens are cast iron, I've seen chefs that swear by each one.

Cast iron is probably the most popular. It's the historic choice. It heats evenly (if slowly), and it holds the heat well, so your food stays warm in it, even after it's done cooking. It can take a lot of heat without damage too. Unfortunately, it's also heavy, and the bigger the oven, the heavier. Cast iron has to be seasoned (that deep black coating) to be used effectively, but with regular use, that seasoning patina gets better and better, and it becomes nonstick. Cast iron also lasts forever.

Aluminum Dutch ovens are much lighter than cast iron, so it's often the pot of choice for campers, river runners, and backpackers that carry their gear in to their campsites. It won't rust, so you don't need to season it. It heats up quickly, but that also means that it cools quickly, and it's prone to developing hot spots.

Some say that cast iron–cooked food tastes better, but I've tasted delicious food from both kinds.

THE QUALITY

The best Dutch ovens I've ever seen come from three companies: Lodge, Camp Chef, and Maca. There are lots of littler brands, like Texsport, and a few that are even no-name. You can often come across Dutch ovens at yard sales and antique stores. Some Dutch oven chefs I know will swear by one brand or another. While it's true that there are some that are better made, keep in mind that our pioneer ancestors cooked successfully in Dutch ovens made hundreds of years before modern companies were formed and contemporary casting procedures were invented. I've cooked delicious meals in off-brand Dutch ovens. I prefer my Lodge, but you can be successful with anything.

Here are some hints to check the quality:

First, check to see that the lid fits well. Press down on the lip of the lid all the way around. If you find a spot where the lid rocks back and forth, that's a sign of a poorly fitting lid. That will let more moisture escape when you're cooking. Again, you can still cook well in that pot, but it won't be quite as effective.

Some off-brands will use different alloys or different sources for their cast iron stock. That can make for variations in the thickness of the pot and the density of the metal. In either case, that can make for uneven heating and hotspots. Unfortunately, you can't really check for that in the store. It's one reason why you might want to go with a more respected brand.

Still, my forefathers that crossed the plains didn't have a Lodge or a Camp Chef.

SUMMING IT ALL UP

Okay, so this is really a seventy-five-dollar answer to a ten-dollar question. What Dutch oven should I buy? My recommendation is that if you're wanting to get started in outdoor Dutch oven cooking, get a 12-inch, shallow Lodge or Camp Chef. You'll possibly notice that almost all of the recipes in my blog use that basic size. My two 12-inchers are the workhorses of my cast iron collection.

Whatever you end up buying, now you have some knowledge to help you make a wise choice, either to get started or to expand once you've gotten a few recipes down.

DUTCH OVEN FRIED CHICKEN, WRAPPED IN BACON

Jodi and I were attending a local expo, and there were some cooking demonstrations going on. I, of course, was enthralled. Jodi, not so much. But she sat there and endured it, and when the chef was all done and she sampled what he'd been cooking, she was enthralled too. We exchanged glances, and it was clear to both of us what I'd be cooking for Sunday dinner that week!

Sometimes, people pick chicken recipes because they're healthy and low fat. They might want to trim a few pounds. To those good folks, I say . . .

Skip this one and go on to the next! This one has been officially condemned by numerous heart health organizations. It's *evil*! RUN! Turn the page quickly!

TOOLS
12-inch Dutch oven
18–22 coals below, no coals above, lid off
You'll also need some wooden skewers.

INGREDIENTS
1–1½ lbs. boneless, skinless chicken breasts (about one piece per serving)
1 lb. thick-sliced, peppered bacon (you can use thin, unpeppered, if you must)
salt
juice of 2–3 lemons

THIS ONE was so simple it was almost embarrassing. But it is soo, sooo good.

I used frozen boneless, skinless chicken breasts. The chef at the expo used chicken tenderloins. If I'd had any, I probably would have too, because they're already the size and shape you need. As it was, I had to use breasts.

I thawed them, and once they were thawed, I lit up the coals. Once they were ready, I got the coals under the Dutch oven, with just a quick spritzing of oil inside the oven. That's not really necessary, but it helps the chicken to not stick at first. The bacon will eventually fully grease up the Dutch oven.

I came in and sliced the chicken into thirds in long, thick strips. Again, the tenderloins are already shaped that way. Then I picked up a skewer and a strip of bacon and poked through one end of the bacon strip. I skewered through the chicken piece so the skewer ran through the length of the chicken and came out the other end. I wrapped the bacon tightly around the chicken to about halfway, when the strip ran out. Then, I stuck another piece of bacon on the skewer on the other end, and wound it tightly back to the middle. I shaped it a bit with my hand, and it stayed in place pretty well.

Finally, I broke off the skewer so that there wasn't much wood on either end of the chicken, just enough to hold the bacon in place. I stacked these chicken bits up.

23

I brought them all out and put them into my Dutch oven. I had to squeeze them in really tight like good friends. I repeated that process until I ran out of either chicken strips or bacon strips. In this case, I had one strip of chicken left over, and no room left in the Dutch oven.

This is really so simple, because really, I was using the Dutch oven as if it were a skillet.

If you've heated up the Dutch oven right, it should crackle and sizzle right away when you put in the chicken. Bit by bit, I turned them with a short set of tongs. (Please don't use the same tongs you used for the coals!) Let them cook pretty well on each side before turning them, because that helps the bacon to stay in place. This time I was impatient, and some of the pieces unraveled a bit.

After they'd been cooking on a couple of sides, I got out the lemons and splattered some juice over the chicken pieces. That, of course, set up new waves of sizzling and a luscious new wave of smells to mix with the bacon, chicken, and pepper. Finally, after 20–30 minutes, they were done, and I brought them in.

It was way, way delicious and so simple. You can't go wrong with this one.

ZEN ON THE COB IN THE DUTCH OVEN

I like fancy. I like complex. I like a challenge. I like to see if I can pull off intricate dishes and stretch myself. I like to take simple dishes and enhance them—to "kick them up a notch."
"Ba-bam" and all that.

This weekend, however, I got to cook something incredibly basic, and it tasted wonderful.

We were having a big barbecue party for a lot of Jacob's teachers and support staff at his school, and I spent a lot of time at the grill, naturally. But on the side, I made some steamed corn on the cob. It was so simple that I'm not even going to spell it out in a recipe.

I started by lighting a lot of coals and pouring about half of them (I'm guessing about 20 or more) onto my cooking surface. I put a veggie steamer (one of those metal fan-out things) in the bottom of my 12-inch, deep Dutch oven. I poured in water until it was just up to the level of the steamer and then laid the corn cobs (shucked and snapped in half) onto it. Then I put the Dutch oven on the coals.

Pretty soon, it was venting steam a little, so I knew it was boiling. I just kept fresh coals on for 30–45 minutes, until the corn looked yellow and cooked—you know, like corn on the cob is supposed to. Then we served it up with butter, salt, and pepper. Yum! Only two pieces were left over when it was all done.

Sometimes, simple and pure is perfect, right? Zen—on the cob!

FRESH DUTCH OVEN CHICKEN NOODLE SOUP

I really like roasting chickens. One chicken is just about enough meat for our small family, and there are so many wonderful ways of seasoning it. You can find a lot of my own experiments in the poultry chapter. One of the really cool things about roasting a whole bird is that you never get all the meat off when you're serving it up. That means that the next day, you can make the most incredible soup (or stock) you've ever tasted.

Chicken bouillon cubes? Pfft! Only in the direst of emergencies!

Well, I suppose that you can use bouillon or stock-in-a-box if you want to. It's better than nothing. I guess . . .

This particular soup was made the day after cooking a wonderful chicken for my anniversary. Elegant and delicious, and the next day, the celebration continues!

TOOLS
12-inch, shallow Dutch oven
lots of coals below, replenished

INGREDIENTS
1 formerly 5-lb. chicken carcass
2–3 stalks celery, sliced
1 large onion, sliced
1–2 large carrots, sliced
about ¼ cup lemon juice
salt and pepper
1 pkg. egg noodles

I STARTED out by putting the carcass of the previous day's roast into the 12-inch, shallow Dutch oven, with about 2–3 inches of water. I had lit up a lot of coals, and I shook them out of the chimney and arranged them on my little metal cooking table. The carcass and the water went into that Dutch oven, covered.

After about a half hour, it was boiling away. I let it boil for a long time, simmering the meat and the bones into a delicious stock.

Finally, I pulled the Dutch oven off the coals. I took the bones of the chicken and picked off as much meat as I could. The meat I put back into the broth. The broth, by the way, was permeated with all the spices and herbs that I'd used the previous day. If you don't have the remains of a picked-over chicken to boil up, you can cube up some frozen chicken breasts and boil them to make the broth. If you do, then add some of the herbs that I used originally. Or any others that you want to add yourself.

Go for it.

It's your soup, ya know.

Then, with just the meat and the broth left, I put that back on the coals and came inside to slice up the veggies. Those went into the pot. I let the veggies cook for a while. Once they were soft, I added the noodles.

If it's too runny for your taste, add a touch of flour, starch, or cream of tartar and stir it all up. Then pull it off and serve it! Yum!

COOKING A WHOLE MEAL

Now that you've tried a few basic dishes, let's put a few of them together in an article that I've titled, "How to Cook Your First Outdoor Dutch Oven Meal—Without Fail and Without Stress!" The recipes may well be found in other pages of this same book, but I'm going to reprint them here so that you can access them all in one spot.

Maybe you've just gotten a Dutch oven, and maybe you've even cooked a thing or two in it. Or maybe you're just wanting to. It can be a bit overwhelming to think of all the things you could cook.

But let's say that you want to do a camp or backyard meal. Not just one dish, but a full meal that everyone in your family or group can enjoy. Let's plan it and do it up right.

First, we're dealing with cooking multiple things at once, so we're going to make each thing very simple. If you try to do several difficult dishes at once, it gets exponentially more complex. Believe me, I've done it. It ain't pretty.

We're going to do three dishes: A bread, a main dish, and a dessert. The bread will be a garlic butter drop biscuit, the main dish will be a one-pot chicken-and-potatoes dish, and the dessert will be a "dump cake" peach cobbler.

TOOLS YOU NEED

At least one, but up to three 10- or 12-inch camp-style Dutch ovens (the ones with the legs). They'd have to be seasoned. If you have three, you can cook all of the dishes concurrently. If you have only one, you'll have to cook them one at a time.

A lid lifter (could be a fancy one, or even the claw end of a hammer)

One 20-lb. bag of charcoal (preferably normal Kingsford)

Long-handled tongs for placing and moving lit coals

Kitchen spoons, knives, chopping boards, and so on

Bowls for mixing, serving, and so on

Gloves for handling a hot Dutch oven

INGREDIENTS

The Biscuits
2 cups biscuit mix (like Bisquick)
²/₃ cup milk or buttermilk
½ cup cheddar cheese, shredded
½ cup butter
¼ tsp. garlic powder
dried parsley, chopped

The Chicken and Potatoes
a few Tbsp. olive oil
2–3 medium to large onions, sliced
3–4 boneless chicken breasts, cubed
3–4 potatoes, quartered and sliced
2–3 carrots, sliced
3–4 stalks of celery, sliced
2–3 sweet peppers, sliced
about a half pound of bacon, cooked crispy
1 heaping Tbsp. minced garlic
liberal shakes parsley, rosemary, oregano
a few shakes (about a tsp. or so) balsamic vinegar.
and, of course, salt and pepper

The Dump Cake
1 18-oz. box yellow cake mix
2 16-oz. cans of peaches
4 Tbsp. butter
¼ cup brown sugar
cinnamon

LET'S ASSUME that you have only one Dutch oven. You'll make the biscuits first, then the main dish. Finally, just before you're serving and enjoying the two, you'll put the dump cake together, and it will be done as people are ready for dessert.

STEP 1: Begin by lighting a stack of 35 or 40 coals. Once you count those out on your oven, you'll have extra, but you'll use those to light more coals! While they're lighting up, use your tongs to stir them up a bit so they all heat evenly. Spread a little oil or butter around the inside of your Dutch oven.

Once the coals are all a bit white, put 11 coals in a ring around the legs of the Dutch oven and put another 22 on the lid, in a ring around the edge. Let it heat up the Dutch oven.

STEP 2: Mix the biscuit mix, milk, and cheese. Sprinkle in some garlic salt, if you'd like.

STEP 3: Once the Dutch oven is hot, lift off the lid and drop the biscuit dough in by large spoonfuls around the bottom of the Dutch oven. Put the lid back on and let them bake for 15–20 minutes, or until they're nice and golden.

STEP 4: While the biscuits are baking, blend together the butter, the garlic salt, and the parsley. If you can melt the butter, that's great.

STEP 5: Also, while the biscuits are baking, you can chop and slice up the veggies for the main dish.

STEP 6: Right before the biscuits are done, pour some more coals (about 25) on top of the still-burning leftover coal pile. Stir those up so the fresh coals will get lit.

STEP 7: Pull the biscuits out of the Dutch oven and onto a plate. Spread the butter mix liberally onto them and let it melt in, if it's not already melted. Then, put those biscuits in a bowl or basket lined with a towel to keep them as warm as possible.

STEP 8: Wipe the crumbs out of the Dutch oven, put a little oil on the bottom, and put it back on the coals. Finish chopping up the veggies and cubing the chicken and put all of the main dish ingredients into the Dutch oven. Put on the lid.

You won't need as much heat for this dish. It's likely that many of the original coals will be burning down by now. You'll want about 8 coals on the bottom and 17 on the top. You can put on more if the weather is cold.

Cook this for 45 minutes to an hour until the chicken is all done and the potatoes are soft. Stir it about every 15 minutes.

STEP 9: If your supply of coals is burning low, either in the pile or on the pot, replenish it.

STEP 10: Serve the biscuits and the main dish. As soon as you're done serving, put any remaining chicken and potatoes into a bowl and clean out the Dutch oven. Scrape it with a plastic spatula or a plastic brush and rinse it out with hot water, not cold!

STEP 11: Pour in the cans of peaches, Then sprinkle the cake mix on top. Scatter the brown sugar and cinnamon over the cake mix and put 4–5 pats of butter on top of it all.

STEP 12: Put the Dutch oven back on the coals, with 10–12 coals below and 10–12 coals above. Bake it for about 45 minutes, while everyone eats and rests with the main dish.

STEP 13: Serve up the dessert!

Now, if you have two Dutch ovens, you could cook the biscuits first and do the main dish and the dessert at the same time. Or you could cook the biscuits and the chicken and potatoes at the same time, and the dessert last. If you have three Dutch ovens, you could do them all overlapped.

By following these simple steps, you will have cooked a full meal, entirely out-doors, in your Dutch ovens. Low stress, and a delicious meal!

CHAPTER 2
BEEF

I REMEMBER once hearing a comedian say that he thought it was funny which animals we thought were acceptable to eat and which ones were not. He postulated that the reason we eat beef and not horse is that, at one point, a horse and a cow were standing next to each other. An early man approached, with his spear. Only the horse was smart enough and quick enough to get away.

It could be. I mean, I've never eaten a horse. Have you?

MARK'S LAYERED MEATLOAF

It's not often that I go camping. I don't really object to it, I just don't get much opportunity or have much time for it. But when I do go, it's usually a lot of fun.

As I've mentioned before, most of my Dutch oven cooking happens on my back porch. It's convenient, and I've got my Dutch oven tables, chimney, lid lifters, and other gear stored out there on a relatively permanent basis. Once in a while, however, I do like to go and cook "in the wild." It kinda reminds me of what my ancestors went through.

This one, while not authentic pioneer grub, was once cooked on a campout, called a "Fathers and Sons Campout," sponsored by my church's local congregation. As the name implies, all the dads in the congregation take all their sons camping to the same location. Great time to spend together. Since Jodi was out of town over the weekend, it was good timing too. I also used it as a chance to get more practice cooking at a campsite.

TOOLS
12-inch Dutch oven
8–9 coals below, 16 coals above

31

INGREDIENTS

The Basic Meatloaf
1½ lbs. ground beef
1 large onion, chopped
½ cup bread crumbs (or, better, crushed crackers or croutons)
2 eggs
ketchup or barbecue sauce to taste
salt, pepper, and Worcestershire sauce to taste

The Other Layers
1 lb. medium pork sausage
About 2 cups grated cheddar (I like sharp cheddar, but it's also good with other yellow
  cheeses, like Colby or Colby-Jack.)

I STARTED by setting some coals on to burn, then I chopped up the onions. I had forgotten any kind of worktable, so I had to improvise. I just put a thin cutting board on top of the food cooler. Then I mixed the ground beef, onion, bread crumbs, eggs, sauces, and spices. You could actually use your own favorite meatloaf recipe if you prefer. I divided it in half.

Then, I spread one half of the beef meatloaf mixture in the bottom of the Dutch oven. Don't worry about greasing the bottom, it'll be plenty greasy on its own. I sprinkled a thin layer of cheddar. I spread the sausage, then another thin layer of cheddar. Finally, I put on a top layer of the rest of the meatloaf mixture and then a last sprinkling of cheddar.

I put it on the coals to bake, and I made sure to turn the oven and the lid about every 15–20 minutes to keep it from burning. I cooked it for about an hour. While it's the best tasting meatloaf I've ever eaten, it's *not* low-fat! I spooned off the drippings before we ate.

This was actually the second time I've made this meatloaf, and I really didn't alter the recipe from the first time. Well, that's not true. The first time, the sausage was hot, and, while I like hot sausage, I found it overpowered the taste of the other meat. So I went with medium this time.

DUTCH OVEN MEATBALLS WITH POTATOES

This one is some yummy comfort food at our house. It's a dish I've made before, and one that my wife used to make a lot (using the indoor oven, especially when we were first married). It's a simple dish, a one-pot, two-step. Easy, yes; delicious, yes; healthy, not so much!

TOOLS
12-inch Dutch oven
8–9 coals below
16–18 coals above
You'll need a side fire, because this one runs over an hour.

INGREDIENTS
1 medium to large onion, sliced
3 cloves garlic, chopped
4–5 green onions, chopped
2–3 sweet peppers, chopped

2 lbs. ground beef
3 slices bread, chopped
2 eggs
salt
pepper
liberal shakes of parsley

½ pkg. cream cheese

4–5 medium potatoes
2 (10.75-oz.) cans cream of mushroom soup
juice of 1 lemon

1 layer grated cheddar

I STARTED off by heating a tablespoon or two of oil in the Dutch oven with about 15–20 hot coals below it. I wanted to get the oil nice and hot to sauté all of the ingredients in the first set.

While that was cooking, I made the meatballs. I mixed everything in the second set and blended it up nicely. Then I made a meat patty about a half inch thick and the size of my palm. I scooped off a piece of cream cheese, about the size of a fingertip. I put that in the middle of the patty and closed the meat around it. The final meatball was just a little larger than a golf ball. I also sliced up the potatoes and opened up the cans of soup.

Back out at the Dutch oven, I arranged the meatballs on top of the now cara-melized veggies, with a little space between each. I scattered in the potato slices between the meatballs, then spooned the soup concentrate from the cans on top. I spritzed on the lemon juice and closed the lid. I set it with 10–12 coals on the bottom and 16–18 on top and let it bake for about an hour, or until the potatoes were nice and soft.

Then I brought it in. I put a layer of grated cheese on top and put the lid back on, letting the cheese melt.

It's yummy, gooey, and oh, so comforting. Love it!

I've also done this served over rice. It's good that way too, but with the potatoes, you don't really need more starch. It's up to you!

DUTCH OVEN BEEF RIBS

My wife and I once joined a local food co-op. It's a kind of interesting way to get food, especially stuff grown and produced locally. We got our first share one Saturday, and that Sunday, I was looking it all over and trying to figure out what I could do with it. One of the meat things that came in our share was two racks of beef ribs, with four bones each. I was surprised just how big beef ribs are, compared to pork ribs (which is what I was most used to having in barbecue).

Anyway, I dug in and did some research, looking for a good recipe and a good process. There were all kinds of methods: grilling, braising, baking, roasting. Some were a combination of two or three methods. One thing seemed consistent: the longer it takes to cook them, the more tender and delicious they are. So I decided to go with "low and slow" cooking.

Finally, after looking at all the options, my wife said, "Grandma Bev used to make the most delicious ribs with this barbecue sauce based on brown sugar, ketchup, and mustard. Why don't you try that?"

In the interests of both nostalgia and simplicity, I decided to give it a try. What I came up with isn't much of a recipe in the traditional sense of the word. It's more of a set of instructions. You can make it work with the things you have on hand.

TOOLS
12-inch Dutch oven
6–7 coals below, 12–15 coals above

INGREDIENTS

The Meat
2–3 racks (4 bones each) of beef ribs

The Veggies
some sliced onions
some sliced green onions
some minced garlic
some halved cherry tomatoes
some sliced celery
and anything else you care to add in. Mushrooms would
  have tasted good too, if I'd had any.

The Sauce
a generous cup brown sugar
ketchup
mustard
salt
pepper
some kind of hot spice (cayenne pepper or chili powder)

I STARTED out prepping the veggies, slicing them up, and so on. I got some coals burning and poured a bunch out on my little Dutch oven table. I put the Dutch oven on the coals, with some olive oil (a couple of tablespoons) to heat up for sautéing.

Once the oil was hot and the veggies sliced, I put the two kinds of onions and the garlic in to sauté. I'd stir it occasionally, but at that point, I turned my attention to the sauce.

I started with a bowl and put in about a cup of brown sugar. From that point on, I went simply by taste. I added some ketchup and some mustard (about even amounts of each) and started tasting. It was weird tasting these condiments cold with nothing to put them on, but I was working out the proportions. In the end, I added more and more mustard. But then, I'm a big mustard fan. Salt brought out the other flavors, and pepper is just great to add to anything, in my opinion. The hot spice I added to just give it an edge. I just went along, adding and tasting, adding and tasting, until I got it to where I wanted it.

And in between that, I was stirring the veggies.

Once the sauce was mixed right, I poured about half of it into a resealable baggie. I cut the ribs apart and added the meat to the baggie. I shook it all up to coat the ribs.

Back out on the Dutch oven, I added the rest of the vegetables and then layered the meat on top.

I adjusted the coals as above. The coals listed above are arranged in a baking configuration. You could probably also do a more roasting sort of arrangement by putting 10–11 coals on the bottom and the same amount on top. Remember that in this case, you'll be cooking with less heat for a longer time, so if you're going to make a mistake, make it on the lower side of the scale.

From that point on, cooking was simply a matter of making sure that there was a constant supply of fresh coals to add on. I cooked the ribs for 2½–3 hours, in total. Wow, they tasted amazingly, fall-off-the-bone good.

DUTCH OVEN ROAST BEEF WITH BALSAMIC GLAZE

A long time ago, I figured out that there are two ways to cook roast beef so that you don't have to chew it forever to be able to swallow it. One way is to cook it medium to medium rare, so that it's still a bit pink and juicy. I like my steaks that way, so it would stand to reason that I also like my roasts that way. I've been able to pull off this kind of roast before.

The other way to cook it is to roast it "low and slow" (meaning at a low temperature, for a long time), and to overcook it. You keep it on the heat until the meat becomes so tender that it falls apart under your fork, and you hardly need a knife to eat it.

This recipe is for the second approach.

SLOW DUTCH OVEN ROAST WITH A BALSAMIC GLAZE

TOOLS
12-inch, deep Dutch oven
8–10 coals below, 10–12 coals above

INGREDIENTS
2 Tbsp. olive oil
3–4 cloves garlic, minced
kosher salt
coarse ground pepper
3- to 5-lb. beef roast
3–4 large potatoes
3–4 medium onions
1–2 carrots, sliced
2–3 stalks celery, sliced

The Glaze
1 Tbsp. coarse ground pepper
1 Tbsp. kosher salt
1 Tbsp. olive oil
3 Tbsp. balsamic vinegar
½ cup honey, maybe a little more
2–3 Tbsp. flour
about ¼ cup water

FIRST OF all, I made sure that the meat was completely thawed from the beginning. That meant the time spent cooking was spent cooking and not melting the meat.

A couple of hints on thawing: I like to thaw meat by putting it in the sink under running water. Make sure that the water's cool. I've done it with hot water, thinking that it would thaw faster. It doesn't, and it actually starts cooking the outer edge of the meat. Another hint is to remove the meat from the packaging and put it in a resealable baggie before putting it in the water. The little styro-foam tray will insulate the meat and keep the bottom side from thawing.

When it was thawed, I coated it with kosher salt and coarse-ground pepper. I let it sit for a while.

Meanwhile, I lit up some coals and preheated the Dutch oven with the oil in it. There were just a lot of coals on the bottom, at first. I tossed in the garlic and let that sauté a little bit, then put the roast in the Dutch oven and browned it for about 4 minutes on each side.

Since I was kinda learning how to do this, I also set a thermometer into it. I closed up the lid and put the proper coals on. My idea was to cook it at 200–250 degrees for 4–5 hours. It took a while, but it eventually got up to 200. From then on, it was just a matter of keeping the heat steady with fresh coals.

I made sure that I kept the coals to a minimum. I kept it hot, but not too hot. The day I did this, there was a pretty steady breeze out, so I had to replace them often. The coal counts of 8–10 below and 10–12 on top were pretty accurate to what I was trying to maintain. I cooked it a total of 5–5½ hours. It reached an internal temperature of "well-done" after about 2½–3 hours. Toward the end, I started testing it by seeing how easily I could pry apart the meat fibers with a pair of forks.

I didn't add any veggies or herbs until about the third hour. I just poured them around the meat. I left the meat on the metal bottom of the oven, rather than lifting it up on a trivet or resting it on the potatoes. I don't know if that made any difference at all, considering the relatively low heat.

I mixed up the glaze and, about an hour out to "done," I started basting it on the top of the meat every 15 minutes or so. It really added a sweet and sharp depth to the flavor of the meat. It also formed a rich crust on some parts of the meat.

About 15 minutes before my projected "done" time, I started ladling off the liquid stock at the bottom of the pot to make a gravy. There really wasn't much liquid to use. In retrospect, I don't really think the meat needed the extra mois-ture nor flavor of a gravy. Still, I made some, and it didn't taste bad.

When I pulled it off the coals, I set it on the table, and we spent a good 15 to 20 minutes gathering and setting the table. That allowed the meat to rest and the juices to redistribute. The residual heat also cooked it just a little bit more.

Finally, when we were all gathered, and the prayer said, I went to serve it, and it just fell apart under the fork. I had brought out a knife to cut it and serve it, but I didn't use it. My kids raved about it. Really, the glaze and the long, slow cook made all the difference.

DUTCH OVEN BACON—DRAPED ROAST BEEF

So, that last recipe was how to cook it "low and slow" to overdone richness. This one is all about cooking it the other way, to a soft and delicate medium doneness.

This approach and recipe came about because I had invited a friend and his family over to celebrate his birthday. We've known each other for years. He's also a musician—a drummer—and we've worked together a lot of times and played in a few bands together. He helped me with the drums on my first CD. I hadn't seen him in a long time, and I was going to prepare a magnificent roast for him.

So, I looked on the Net to find something that would just "wow" to the next level. I found a bunch of great recipes, and after a bit of thinking, I came up with one that would just be amazing. And I was going to throw in an extra touch that would just throw it over the edge. In addition to all the spices and flavorings, I would drape the roasts in thick-sliced bacon!

In the end, my friend, always quick with a quip, sat back and sighed, "Well, that cow sure died with honors!" So, I guess the recipe passed approval.

TOOLS
12-inch, deep Dutch oven
14–16 coals above, 14–16 coals below

I STARTED with a slab of meat to roast. I actually did two that added up to a little over 5 pounds, since I knew we'd be feeding two families. I started the coals and, when they were ready, put some olive oil in the bottom and set the Dutch oven on about 20–25 coals (underneath) to heat up. While that was heating, I prepared the rub.

The Rub
liberal shakes of salt and coarse ground pepper, maybe as much as a Tbsp. of each. I
   used sea salt, but I don't know if that made a difference or not.
2 Tbsp. minced garlic
½ tsp. mustard seed
½ tsp. marjoram
½ tsp. rosemary
½ tsp. thyme
1 Tbsp. parsley

I STIRRED it all up and rubbed it all over the meat. That was a bit messy. Then I put the meat in the oven and let it brown on all sides.

While it was browning, I prepared the liquid. What do you call that for a roast? The sauce? The baste? I'll go with that.

The Baste
1 cup hot beef broth (I used an au jus mix)
3 Tbsp. honey
a couple of liberal shakes soy sauce
a couple of bay leaves
a bit more liberal shakes black pepper. I like it coarse ground.

WHEN I carried the basting liquid out, I brought out the bacon as well. I opened up a 1-pound package. How much of it you actually use will depend on the size and shape of your roast. I like the thick-sliced bacon, myself.

So I poured in the baste. At that point, I pulled the oven off the bottom-only coals. I put 14 coals on the lid and 14 coals below in a circle (I had to pull some from my side fire).

While the roast was cooking, I rested for a while. I figured it would take about 3 hours to cook the roast. I left a thermometer stuck in the meat, so I was able to constantly monitor it. So, after about half that, I chopped up the veggies, stirred them up, and added them. All the while, I maintained my side fire and pulled fresh coals to replenish the ones that were burning out.

The Veggies
2 medium onions, sliced
a bunch of small green onions, sliced
2 stalks celery, sliced
a green bell pepper, sliced
I took a jalapeno and sliced about 6 very thin slices off of it. Then I chopped those
  slices a little.
1 large carrot, sliced
4 medium potatoes, quartered and sliced
A handful of mushrooms, sliced

AT THAT point, everything that was going in was in. It was just a matter of keeping the coals hot and waiting for it to get done.

Soon it was at 140 degrees, or just a little higher. According to the thermometer gauge, that would make it rare. At about 145 degrees, I pulled it off the heat but kept the lid on. As we were setting the table, I let the meat rest and come up to full temperature. I was shooting for 150 degrees, which is a sort of medium doneness.

About the same time, I got out my 8-inch Dutch oven and a ladle. I carefully pulled 1½–2 cups of broth out of the big Dutch oven and poured it into the small one. I arranged about 10 coals packed pretty tight and close and set the 8-incher on top. Then I stirred up some flour into some water. I don't really know how much, maybe a total of 2–3 Tbsp. into about a half cup of water, maybe less. I stirred it up to dissolve the flour and poured it into the broth. I let that sit and boil for a while, stirring it as it got thicker and thicker and became a nice gravy.

Finally it was ready to serve. I just carved it up and served the veggies on the side. I loved it, and we all ate hearty that night.

DINNER IN A PUMPKIN IN A DUTCH OVEN

This dish is traditional for us around mid-fall. Typically, when there's a Halloween party for our group of parents of special needs kids, or a church party, my wife will make this meal. It's really cool because the presentation is seasonal.

The basic idea is that you hollow out the pumpkin and fill it with a seasoned hamburger, rice, veggies, and sauce mix, then bake the whole thing. When you serve it up, the pumpkin itself becomes the serving bowl. You spoon out the meal mix, and as you do, you scrape in some of the baked pumpkin from the sides. The flavors all blend. It's delicious!

And I'm *not* a big fan of gourds and squash!

It does, however, take a few steps and several Dutch ovens to pull it off. If you wanted to, say, cook this for an outdoor event or for camping, you could prepare all of the filling mix in your kitchen beforehand and just do the final bake in the Dutch oven.

TOOLS

12-inch Dutch oven (for browning and sautéing)
8-inch Dutch oven (for rice)
14-inch, deep Dutch oven (for baking the meal)
12 coals below, 22 coals above (maybe a few more if it's a bit cold and windy)

INGREDIENTS

1 cup rice
2 cups water
1–2 Tbsp. olive oil
2 medium onions, chopped or sliced
3–4 stalks celery, chopped
2–3 cloves garlic, minced
1 cup mushrooms, sliced
1 lb. ground beef
1 (10.75-oz) can cream of something soup
salt
pepper
parsley
1 pumpkin, smaller and kinda flat
2 tsp. chili powder
2 tsp. cinnamon
2 Tbsp. brown sugar

I STARTED out by heating up some coals. I got the rice and water cooking in the 8-inch oven and started sautéing the onions, celery, mushrooms, and garlic in the 12-inch. When I cook rice, I just watch it until steam starts venting, then take it off the coals about 10 minutes after that. Then I let it sit with the lid on for about another 10 minutes. It usually works, and doesn't burn the rice on the bottom. When you're sautéing veggies, you want the oven to be pretty hot, enough that the oil in the bottom looks shimmery and the veggies sizzle the moment they hit the pan.

Once the veggies were looking a bit caramelized, I added the ground beef and browned it.

While that was cooking, I prepared the pumpkin. The first time I cooked this in my Dutch ovens, it was a challenge to pick the right pumpkin. I had to get out my tape measure and measure the inside of the 14-inch Dutch oven and then measure all of the pumpkins at the store. I must've looked pretty funny walking around measuring each one! I felt a little like Linus from *Peanuts*, making sure that his pumpkin patch was sincere enough for the Great Pumpkin.

I found one that was kinda flat when laid on its side, yet I realized that there was no way it would fit into the oven. It was still too tall. So, I just decided to cut it into a bowl shape and move on.

What I did was place the pumpkin in the Dutch oven and, using a knife, mark the "lid level" all the way around the pumpkin. Then I took it out and cut the top off, using that knife mark as a guide. That set the precedent, and now that's how I do it every time I cook this.

Finally, I hollowed out the seeds and scraped off the fibrous parts inside the pumpkin. Then I got out the chili powder, cinnamon, and brown sugar and mixed those together. I sprinkled that around the inside. I tried to get all up the sides as well. Turning and shaking the pumpkin helps. If you have to mix up more, that's fine. The idea is to coat the inside of the pumpkin. I sometimes rub it in, but you don't really have to, because the moisture from the pumpkin rind will pretty much help it absorb and keep the spices in place.

Then I brought in all the other Dutch ovens and mixed their contents together with the can of soup and the seasonings. I poured this glop into the pumpkin and placed it into the 14-inch, deep Dutch oven. If I do the measuring right, the lid fits nicely!

I put that oven out on the coals for almost two hours. I kept sticking the pumpkin rind with thin bamboo skewers, and when I felt little resistance, I knew it was soft and ready to serve.

That first time, my kids kept saying that they wouldn't eat the pumpkin, but they both did. A good way to get kids to eat squash, right? It was a real treat, and it's fun to see the food coming right out of the pumpkin.

I've thought that one time I do this, I'm going to try it with the Dutch oven upside down. That is, I'll put the lid on the bottom, on a lid stand over the coals, and put the body of the Dutch oven on top, with coals around the legs. That way, when I serve, the lid will look like a tray, and the pumpkin won't be hidden down in the oven.

ADDITIONAL FAMILY RECIPES

SHEPHERD'S PIE

TOOLS
12-inch Dutch oven
20+ coals below for boiling
8 coals below, 16 coals above for baking

INGREDIENTS
5 medium potatoes
lots of water
½ cup milk
½ cup sour cream
1–2 lbs. beef, ground or stew
1–2 medium onions, diced
3–4 cloves garlic, chopped
salt
pepper
1–2 (14.5-oz.) cans tomatoes
1–2 (14.5-oz.) cans green beans and/or corn, drained
1 cup grated cheese

START BY heating up the water. While that's heating up, peel and cube the potatoes. Boil the potatoes until they're soft. Drain the Dutch oven and, in a separate bowl, mash the potatoes. Add the milk and sour cream and stir it up until it's fluffy. Set this aside.

Put the Dutch oven back on the coals and brown the beef, onion, and garlic, seasoned with salt and pepper. Add the tomatoes, green beans, and corn.

Spread the mashed potatoes over the top. Sprinkle on the cheese and bake for about 40 minutes.

SAUCY BEEF AND NOODLES

TOOLS
12-inch Dutch oven
16 coals below
10-inch Dutch oven
16 coals below

INGREDIENTS
¼ cup flour
1½ tsp. paprika
¼ tsp. pepper
¼ tsp. salt
½ tsp. celery seed

2- to 3-lb. roast, cubed
2 Tbsp. oil
½ cup red wine or cranberry juice

1 Tbsp. balsamic vinegar
2 medium onions
3–4 stalks celery, sliced

1 (10.75-oz.) can cream of mushroom soup

water
1 (1-lb.) bag egg noodles

START BY mixing the first set of ingredients in a plastic resealable bag. Add the meat and shake it to coat. Let it sit for a few minutes while the coals heat the oil in the Dutch oven.

Brown the meat in the Dutch oven with the oil. Remove the meat. Use the wine or the cranberry juice to loosen the fond at the bottom of the Dutch oven, scraping with a plastic or wooden scraper.

Add the next set of ingredients and put the meat back in the Dutch oven. Add the soup concentrate and stir it all up. Let it cook "low and slow."

Put some water in the 10-inch Dutch oven, put it over the coals, and when it boils, cook the noodles.

When it's all done, serve the meat and veggies over the noodles.

CHAPTER 3
POULTRY

I DON'T think there's a meat that's as amazingly versatile as chicken. You can do almost anything with it, and it will come out tasting great! The joke goes that "anything tastes like chicken," right? I think that's because you can make chicken taste like almost anything.

HERB ROASTED CHICKEN

The day I first did this one was my twenty-first wedding anniversary! That means that twenty-one years before, in Salt Lake City, my wife accepted me, and for reasons that I'm still not sure of, hadn't kicked me to the curb yet. This anniversary was kinda special for us, because a good friend of ours got married that Saturday in the same temple. All the time I was there, and at the reception, I kept thinking back to our wedding. At the reception, the groom asked me to sing a couple of my songs, so I did a few that I wrote for Jodi. One of them, "The Summer of '87" is a celebration of the memories from the summer leading up to our wedding.

But I digress . . .

I wasn't sure what I was going to cook that week. Our family finances had been pretty stretched out recently, and it'd been difficult. That meant I couldn't go out and splurge on all kinds of fancy ingredients. But still, I wanted to cook some things for our anniversary. My wife had bought a whole chicken for cooking, so I thought it would be fun to roast it.

And, of course, once the roast chicken is carved, then you gotta make stock and soup out of the carcass. So, it'd been a chicken weekend!

TOOLS
12-inch, deep Dutch oven
12–13 coals below, 13–14 coals above

INGREDIENTS

1 roasting chicken (about 5 lbs)
pepper
salt

2 large potatoes, quartered and sliced
1 large onion, sliced
2–3 stalks celery with leaves, sliced
1–2 crumbled bay leaves
salt and pepper

½ cup butter, melted
parsley
rosemary
thyme
minced garlic
juice of 1 lime

I STARTED with the chicken itself. I thawed it thoroughly first, of course. After unwrapping it and shaking out all the liquid, I gave it a light coating of salt and pepper. I set that into the center of the 12-inch, deep Dutch oven. Around that, I added all the sliced veggies and all the stuff in the second set of ingredients. I really should pay attention to exactly how much of each herb and spice I include, but I don't. I just shake some in. I'm learning that you should really just be liberal with them.

Somewhere in all that preparation, I took a minute to go outside and light up some coals.

The next step was to make the baste out of the third set of ingredients. I got out my basting brush and slathered that onto the chicken. I like to poke holes in the chicken skin too to let the baste seep down into the meat more.

With the chicken and veggies all prepared, I put that Dutch oven on the now-hot coals.

From then on, it was simply a matter of keeping fresh coals on the chicken. I would open up the Dutch oven every 15–20 minutes and slap on some more basting sauce. It cooked pretty steadily for 2–2½ hours. I stuck a small meat thermometer in the breast and cooked it to 190 degrees. I looked it up, and the chart Jodi found said it was done at 180, but I just hadn't been paying attention, and it got all the way up to 190. I hope I'm not in trouble for that!

Then I just carved up the bird and served it with the potatoes and vegetables that cooked alongside it. It was delicious! Moist and tender. That's one thing

I love about cooking birds in the Dutch oven. The lid traps the steam, so the meat doesn't dry out.

I saved the bones and the leftover meat for the next day, when I made the chicken noodle soup (p. 26) that's in the Easy Dutch Oven Cooking chapter, here in this very book.

DUTCH OVEN TOMATO—BRAISED CHICKEN

I found this one in a cookbook of mine, and I really liked the appeal of it. It looked a little bit fancier than just roasting up a bird, so I thought I'd give it a try. As always, I tweaked up the recipe a little bit, based on my experience long ago of making tomato soup from scratch.

This one's a two-step process. You first cook the bird and the veggies in the Dutch oven with the liquid and let the tomatoes dissolve. Then you carve the bird and purée the liquid with a little thickener to make the sauce. Finally, you serve it up together.

And then, the next day, I had enough leftover chicken bits and sauce to make a delicious, thick soup. It really was a versatile meal.

TOOLS
12-inch, deep Dutch oven
10–12 coals below, 12–14 coals above

INGREDIENTS
1 whole chicken
salt
black pepper
cayenne
4–5 stalks celery, chopped
4–5 large tomatoes, diced
2 bell peppers, diced
1–2 onions, diced
4–5 cloves garlic, coarsely minced, or sliced
¼ cup lemon juice
2 cups chicken stock
liberal shakes of parsley
liberal shakes of cilantro
2–3 Tbsp. flour

SO, I started off with the chicken, thawed completely, of course. I've had problems with cooking chickens and turkeys that were still frozen. I coated it with kosher salt, coarse ground black pepper, and a little bit of ground cayenne. Keep it light on the cayenne. I don't mind hot, but it can easily overpower the other flavors. I rubbed all that onto the chicken and set it in the deep Dutch oven to allow the seasonings to absorb a bit.

While that was happening, I lit up some coals and started chopping the veggies. I just scattered these all around the chicken, waiting in the Dutch oven. Then I added the juice and stock and sprinkled the herbs on top.

This particular day, I had a really tough time getting coals lit. My wife had bought a bargain brand, and they would *not* light and turn white, no matter what I tried. I did finally get them going, but it took me about an hour to get enough to get started. Lesson learned: Stick with brands you know. My favorite is Kingsford.

The rest of the cooking process was pretty simple. Just keep hot coals on it until the internal temperature reaches 170 degrees or so. There wasn't much else to it. The liquid simmered the veggies down and seasoned the meat, and it was all great. I tasted it a time or two, but I felt it was all pretty balanced.

Once the meat was done, I brought it in and pulled the chicken out of the Dutch oven. That's not always easy for me, because I like to serve straight out of the oven. It's like it connects in my mind that this delicious meal came out of the Dutch oven instead of my stove, and I feel like I've accomplished a greater challenge.

Or something like that.

Anyway, I tented the chicken with some aluminum foil to rest, and I scooped up some of the veggies with a slotted spoon. These, I reserved as a garnish. Then I ladled out most of the remaining liquid and soft veggies into my blender. I added just a bit of flour as thickener, pulsed it up, then puréed it.

Yes, I used an electrical appliance. Sue me.

I carved up the chicken and put it onto a serving tray, then as a final touch, poured the purée on top and added the veggie bits on the side. It looked really good and tasted gourmet as well. I was quite pleased with myself! Smug, even.

DUTCH OVEN TURKEY TIPS

Before I post up my best Dutch oven turkey recipes, I have a few thoughts on doing turkeys. Hopefully these tips will help your turkey dinners and your holiday feasts be the best they can.

SIZE MATTERS

First of all, when I'm shopping for a turkey, I much prefer smaller birds. I think they cook better, fit in my ovens better, and, overall, are tastier and more tender than their bloated, overgrown counterparts. I've come to this conclusion over time, and some of the stories you'll read below are examples of doing huge birds. That's all part of the experience that has taught me that I prefer the 12- to 16-pound hens instead of the 18- to 20-pound toms. More on that to come.

BRINING

I discovered this time-honored technique watching a cooking show once, and I decided to try it. Once you go brine, you'll never go back. Not only does it infuse the turkey with more flavor, but it also helps with a nice, slow, steady thaw. It is a lot more work, but it's worth it. Trust me.

The Brine
1 still-frozen turkey
1 lb. salt
1 lb. brown sugar
lots of water
sometimes a big bag of ice

The night before I'm going to cook a bird, I make up this mix. I start with some hot tap water (maybe a gallon or so) and dissolve the salt and sugar. I let that cool.

Then I clean out a big, portable food cooler we have. I spray the inside with a bit of diluted vinegar to help kill the germs. I take the turkey out if its packaging and put it in, then pour the cooled brine liquid over it. Then I fill it up with water until the turkey's covered. Not so much that it floats, however.

If it's any time but winter, I'll add some ice as well, just to ensure that the whole thing stays cool enough overnight to prevent germs from growing. In the winter, I'll usually put it out in the garage, which is typically around 30 to 35 degrees anyway.

The next day, the turkey is ready for cooking.

COOKING

Because you'll often end up with variations in the temperature of your Dutch oven over the time that you're cooking, I prefer not to decide when it's done based on how long I've been cooking it. I use an approximation to plan the meal, but the final decision on serving is done based on temperature. That magical number is 180 degrees.

Also, measure that with a thermometer inserted into the breast and the thigh, not with the inaccurate and shallow measurement of the little plastic pop-up indicator.

Once it's done, pull it off the coals and let it sit for an additional 15–20 minutes. This can be done in or out of the Dutch oven. Use that time to make the gravy, set the table, pull the guys away from the game, and so on.

BROWNING

One of the reasons that I love to cook turkeys in Dutch ovens is that the heavy lid traps the moisture and the steam. I'm always getting complimented on how moist and tender the birds I cook are.

However, because there's so much steam, you'll not get the skin brown and crisp, at least not all the way around. I've found that the top (the breast), which is closest to the lid, will usually brown and crisp up pretty nicely. Other parts, not so much. I find it's all still quite delicious.

Always remember, after you're all done, that you can make the most delicious turkey stock the next day. There'll be more on this later.

HOLIDAYS

I don't know how turkeys came to be the traditional celebratory meat of the Thanksgiving and Christmas holidays. It could be that they feed a lot of people, and they were probably plentiful in America as those traditions were beginning. But don't wait for Christmas to do a turkey. I like to cook them up all year long. Any time you're having friends over, a bird is always delicious and impressive.

BUYING A DUTCH OVEN FOR TURKEY COOKING

One day, I got an email from someone asking about buying a Dutch oven to cook a turkey. Rather than just jot off a quick recommendation, I wrote out the treatise you see here:

There are a lot of options, and which you'll end up using depends a lot on what you want to do, and especially how big a turkey you want to cook.

My first thought is to get a 14-inch, deep Dutch oven. It's surprising, but that can actually cook a pretty big bird, if that's what you want to do. I have two 14-inch, deep Dutch ovens from some minor brand. My preference is to cook turkey hens in them (which are usually 10–14 pounds). That gives you plenty of room around the bird for air circulation and some veggies, like potatoes, celery, carrots, onions, and so on.

I have, however, also used them at times to cook bigger birds, even up to 22 pounds. Once, when cooking a big one, I had to give it CPR to get the lid to close, but it worked. That also meant that I didn't use a stuffing, and there was no room for veggies around it (which I always like).

There are some additional options for cooking large turkeys. One is the Maca oval Dutch ovens (found at macaovens.com). These are nice and huge. Warning: they are heavy. I've used one before, because I was cooking for all of my wife's family at Christmas. I had to borrow it, and I'm really glad I did. It worked really well, and I'm grateful to the trusting soul that loaned it to me. It will cook a really large turkey. The Dutch oven alone, without the turkey, weighs about 65 pounds. It's truly a beautiful sight to behold.

Another option is the Camp Chef Ultimate Turkey Roaster. This is kind of an oddity in the Dutch oven world. It turns the turkey on its end rather than resting it on its back, as is usual. It's like having two big pots, and you're stacking one on top of the other. I've never used one, but I've seen people do it, and I've seen them cook 20-pound or bigger turkeys in it.

So, all three options work with large turkeys, although the Maca and the Camp Chef Ultimate Turkey Roaster would probably work better.

After all of my experiences cooking turkey, I think the way I'll do it from now on, honestly, is to stick to smaller birds in my 14-inch. I think the smaller turkeys are juicier and tastier. Alton Brown, of the show *Good Eats* on Food Network, agrees with me. He says that the bigger turkeys are raised in small cages, are pumped with hormones or other chemicals, and can barely support their own weight.

If I'm cooking for a crowd, like my in-laws, I can do two 14-pounders, cook them with different, unique seasonings and flavors, and actually have more meat than one 22-pounder with one flavor. Or I can do one turkey and one ham. With smaller birds in two 14-inch Dutch ovens, I have more flexibility and better meat. And I don't have to heft around huge Dutch ovens, either.

Win-win!

So, once again, we have a seventy-five-dollar answer to a ten-dollar question.

Now let's get to some recipes!

DUTCH OVEN CITRUS THANKSGIVING TURKEY

I got the idea for this one while watching the Food Network. Up until then, I had pretty much planned on doing the usual herbal thang that I've been doing in my 14-inch Dutch oven for the last few Thanksgivings. But when I saw them stuffing oranges and lemons in the body cavity, I got really intrigued.

Unfortunately, when I went back a few days later, I couldn't find the recipe. I'd forgotten the show I'd seen it on and the name of the chef who demonstrated it. Still, the Net is huge, and after a few searches and a bit of experimenting, I arrived at my usual conglomeration of ingredients, pulled from many different recipes.

The results were staggering. It was moist and tender (most of the time Dutch oven turkeys are), and the delicate hint of lemon and citrus throughout the meat was especially tasty. My guests (excellent chefs in their own right) pronounced it delicious, and my wife said it was the best turkey she'd ever tasted.

TOOLS
14-inch Dutch oven
12–13 coals below, 22–24 coals above

INGREDIENTS
11- to 13-lb. hen turkey

The Baste
1/2 cup softened butter
1 Tbsp. garlic
zest and juice of 1 lemon
1/8 cup chives or green onions
1/8 cup chopped fresh parsley
a big pinch of kosher salt
liberal shakes of coarse ground pepper

The Stuffing
1 lemon, cut into pieces
1 orange, cut into pieces
1/2 medium onion, diced

The Surrounding Veggies
1 large potato, quartered and sliced
1/2 medium onion, sliced
1/2 cup baby carrots or sliced carrots
3–4 stalks celery, sliced
1/8 cup chives or green onions
1/8 cup chopped fresh parsley

On Top of It All
1–2 sliced citrus fruits (lemons, oranges, grapefruit)
more kosher salt
more coarse ground black pepper

DISCLAIMER: When I first did this recipe, it was before I had discovered the joyous results of brining. If I were to do it now, I would brine it the night before. Instead, I pulled the turkey out of the freezer and put it into the fridge for a few days before Thanksgiving. It was getting soft but was still quite frozen the night before, so I put it in my kitchen sink to fully thaw overnight. Even still, there were some frosty parts deep inside when I went to put in my stuffing.

I STARTED off lighting up a lot of coals. You can see from the header, there, that we're talking around 40, just to get it started. Once it was cooking, I developed a system of transferring over new coals as the old ones burned off that worked pretty well. More on that in a minute.

In the kitchen, first, I cut open the turkey bag and let it drain. I put it onto a towel on my kitchen counter. Then I made the baste. I put the softened butter in a bowl and zested up a lemon. I added that and the juice to the butter, as well as the garlic and so on. It was pretty easy to mix. I also cut up the stuffing items and got those ready.

The stuffing step was pretty easy. I just packed it full, alternating between the lemons, the onions, and the oranges. I pressed it in pretty tight, partly to get more there and partly to squeeze it a bit to get more juices flowing from the fruits. Then I put that into my 14-inch Dutch oven.

I took my baste and coated the top of the bird with it. I like to poke holes in the skin to allow the baste and the seasonings to seep in. Then I sprinkled it with more kosher salt (I like the bigger granules) and the pepper.

I cut up the surrounding veggies and packed those in surrounding the bird. Finally, I added the slices of citrus on top. To keep the citrus from sliding off the turkey, I stuck them in place using toothpicks. It was ready for the coals.

In some ways, this qualifies as a basic Dutching dump meal, because you really do just put everything in and then cook it on the coals. But because there's so much in the management of the heat over such a long period of time, I'd hesitate to call it "basic."

I cooked it to 180 degrees, measured by thermometer. When you take it off the coals, bring it in for everyone to ooh and aah and sniff over, and let it sit for 10–15 minutes. That'll finish off the cooking and let the meat settle into the juices and the seasonings.

Now, not long after I first did this, my wife's family heard her raving about the citrus turkey I'd cooked for my side of the family. Well, they wanted to have the same thing at the Christmas party. I was cool to do it.

Then her stepdad said he would buy the turkey and got a 22-pounder. That's okay, but it was too big. I wasn't sure how I was going to do it. I'd looked into buying one of those Maca big, deep, oval ovens that I mentioned before. They look so cool. Since they're oval, they're perfect for turkeys.

So, I got on the International Dutch Oven Society message board, from idos .org, and asked if anyone had one they would loan. Within a day, I got a response. We communicated and made the connection to pick it up. We got to corresponding and visiting online. So, not only did I get to use a Dutch oven, but I also got a new friend.

Jodi's family was impressed not only with the food but also that someone would loan that out to someone they'd met online. I already knew, though, that Dutch oven people are such cool people.

DUTCH OVEN SPICY TURKEY

One day, when I was contemplating making a turkey for our family, I tried an experiment. Instead of herbs and butter or tangy citrus, I wanted to go southwest and make it spicy. I didn't have any guidelines or any recipes to model it after, so I just made it all up in my head. It was then, and to this day still is, my favorite way to cook turkey.

It's bold and daring, so it's not everyone's favorite, but it is mine!

TOOLS
14-inch Dutch oven
16–18 coals below, 17–19 coals above

INGREDIENTS
1 9- to 12-lb. turkey hen

½ Tbsp. cayenne pepper
½ Tbsp. paprika
½ Tbsp. salt
½ Tbsp. pepper
zest of 1 lemon
juice of 1 lemon
a handful of fresh cilantro, chopped
4–5 green onions, chopped up into the green
2 tsp. cumin
oil, to make a paste

I STARTED by thawing the turkey (again, subsequent times that I've done this recipe, I've done the brining the night before). Before putting it in the Dutch oven, I drained it to be as dry as possible and poked some holes in the skin all over. Then I greased the interior of the Dutch oven and put the turkey in.

I got a small bowl and mixed in all of the ingredients in the second set. The amounts I listed here are approximate; I just grabbed them and shook. I stirred it all up and just adjusted it until it looked and tasted right. It became a sort of red-and-green paste.

I smeared about half of the spice mixture all over the upper surfaces of the turkey. I put it on the breast, the legs—everywhere it would stick. Then I put the oven on the coals.

I cooked it a long time, until the turkey reached 180 degrees. While it was cooking, each time I would lift the lid to check on it (no more than once every 45 minutes or so), I would slather on more of the paste. Eventually, the turkey developed a delicious, deep brown crust.

Wow. Now, as I write this description again, it makes me want to cook it again this weekend!

PARMESAN–CRUSTED CORNISH HENS

Okay, enough with the turkeys for a while.

I've seen these Cornish hen things in the store millions of times and thought how fun it would be to cook them up. They seem so exotic and different, like little, compact chickens.

In fact, there's this apocryphal story about someone stuffing the body cavity of a turkey with a Cornish hen at a family Thanksgiving gathering and then freaking everyone out when they discover the bird they'd just cooked and eaten was pregnant! I guess in the surprise, everyone forgets that turkeys hatch from eggs and that it's not likely that the turkey would live long with its child taking up all the space that the turkey's essential organs would normally be using . . . or the fact that the "baby" bird was cleaned and plucked . . .

Others do that as a legitimate cooking technique. There's a friend of mine who frequently does a turducken, where he stuffs a Cornish hen into a duck, then stuffs that into a turkey.

But I digress . . .

I looked over the Net to try to find a good recipe. I found lots and had a bit of trouble narrowing it down to one that I wanted to do. I found one that was crusted with a flour, Parmesan, and herbal paste, and I thought I'd try that one. As I made it, I had some trouble getting the paste to stick to the bird, but in the end it worked. The recipe below isn't the exact one from the Web, but I think it will work better, based on my experience. In any case, my wife pronounced it fabulous.

TOOLS
12-inch Dutch oven
18+ coals above, 8–9 coals below

INGREDIENTS
2–3 cornish hens (1 hen serves 2 people)
¾ cup flour
¾ cup finely grated Parmesan cheese
1 pinch salt and coarse ground black pepper
½ tsp. marjoram
½ tsp. oregano
½ tsp. garlic powder
enough olive oil to make a paste

I STARTED by thawing the hens in the sink for hours (I don't know how many) and then taking them out of the plastic packs, draining them, and patting them dry.

I mixed all the other ingredients and then attempted to mud up the hens with the paste. Like I said, I had a difficult time making the paste stay on, but I did finally manage. I tried basting on a bath of whipped egg, but I'm not really sure that helped. I placed the three hens squished side-by-side in my 12-inch, shallow Dutch oven. I put that on the coals for about an hour to an hour and a quarter.

Then, while that was cooking, I made some rice in my 8-inch Dutch oven.

MARK'S DUTCH OVEN "WHATEVER YA GOT" RICE

TOOLS
8-inch Dutch oven
6 coals below, 10 coals above

INGREDIENTS
1 cup rice
2 cups water
fresh parsley, chopped
fresh cilantro, chopped
1 onion, quartered and sliced
chopped green onions
1 stalk celery, sliced
salt
pepper
generous outpouring of lemon juice

I JUST dumped all these things into my little 8-inch Dutch oven and put it on top of the 12-inch with some additional coals on top. It really is a "whatever ya got" dish. If I'd had other veggies, I woulda put them in instead.

I really like the taste of lemon rice under poultry, so I was thinking it would complement really nicely. I was right.

When it was all cooked and came time to serve, the birds were actually more meaty than I'd originally thought when I'd bought them, so I cut each one in half down the spine line. It was actually pretty easy once they were cooked. Then I served the half on top of the bed of rice. It was great!

CREAM CHEESE CHICKEN ROLLS

I made two dishes today. One was a recipe for cashew chicken. After deciding to do it, I realized that I didn't have half the ingredients, including the cashews. So I just sort of muddled through with what I had. It turned out pretty well, all things considered. The second was for au gratin potatoes. They both turned out great.

TOOLS
8-inch Dutch oven
12-inch Dutch oven
lots of coals—once it really gets cooking in the 12-inch Dutch oven, 8–9 below and 16–18 or so above

BUT FIRST, I marinated some boneless, skinless chicken breasts. I did 5. You can really pick up whatever commercial marinade you happen to have. This time, I used a ginger and sesame marinade with some minced garlic and a lot of lemon juice. Italian dressing with some extra seasonings would work great, too. I let that marinate for a couple of hours.

Then, in the 8-inch Dutch oven, with 8 coals below and 8 above, I combined:

1 (8-oz.) pkg. cream cheese
1 cup milk
1 medium onion, finely chopped
1 (2.25-oz.) can mushrooms
1–2 tomatoes, diced
1–2 stalks celery, finely chopped
½ jalapeno, chopped
liberal shakes of grated Parmesan cheese

I LET that simmer until the cream cheese melted.

Then, I took the chicken breasts out of the marinade. I took one and pounded it flat between two sheets of waxed paper. Then I put a couple of spoonfuls of the sauce from the 8-inch Dutch oven in the center of the flattened chicken. I folded it over and secured it with a couple of toothpicks. Then I rolled it in whipped egg and then into crushed crackers. This I set in one of my 12-inch, shallow Dutch ovens. I made four more rolls the same way.

Then I poured the rest of the sauce from the 8-inch Dutch oven over the chicken rolls. In retrospect, I might have saved that and poured it over to serve, after the chicken was done. Not sure.

Anyway, it went on the coals and cooked for about 45 minutes. It turned out really good!

DUTCH OVEN JERK CHICKEN WITH SEASONED BAKED POTATOES

The first time I tried this recipe, I did it as an experiment. It kinda worked that night, but in the months that followed, I tried something similar again and again, so I got a better handle on how to do it. I call it my "dry roasting" technique.

I saw this recipe for jerk chicken, and it was really intriguing. But it's supposed to be grilled or broiled. That means that the marinade dries in place in a sort of glaze. Since Dutch ovens trap the moisture, that wouldn't happen. So I thought to myself, what if I could raise the lid with the heat a bit and let the moisture out? So I lifted the lid on a couple of sticks across the top. I had to put a lot of extra coals on it in order to make it work, because with the lid open, much of the heat was escaping with the moisture.

You have to put many, many more coals on the top, and you have to cook it a bit longer. It does, however, produce that dry glaze, so in the end it worked!

Anyway, here's the recipe:

TOOLS
10-inch Dutch oven
7–8 coals below
16 coals above to start, then 24+ coals above

INGREDIENTS
2 lbs. chicken (I used chicken tenderloins, but I'd also recommend boneless breasts)
3 Tbsp. lime juice
2 Tbsp. sweet juice (I used pineapple)
2 Tbsp. oil
1 tsp. soy sauce
5–6 stalks green onions, chopped
1–2 jalapenos, cored, seeded, and chopped
2 Tbsp. allspice
½ tsp. cinnamon
a shake of nutmeg
2 tsp. thyme
salt
black pepper

I STARTED by mixing all of the ingredients (except the chicken) in the bowl. I put those all in a resealable bag and added the thawed chicken. I shook it all up to get it good and coated and put it in the fridge to marinate.

In the meantime, I started the coals and started working on the potatoes. You can find the recipe for those on page 130 in the "Sides" chapter.

The marinated chicken went into the Dutch oven and onto the coals. I started with the lower number of coals on top for about 15 minutes or so, then I lifted the lid and put some straight sticks across the rim of the Dutch oven. I set the lid back down on those sticks, so there was now a gap. I added all the extra coals to the lid and let it cook a while longer, until the marinade was cooked on like a thick, dried glaze.

It sure tasted great!

ADDITIONAL FAMILY RECIPES

ORANGE CHICKEN

TOOLS
12-inch Dutch oven
12 coals below, 12 coals above

INGREDIENTS
6 boneless chicken breasts
½ tsp. ginger
½ tsp. cinnamon
3–4 whole cloves
salt
pepper
8 oz. orange juice concentrate
1½ cups shredded coconut
cooked rice
2 cups mandarin orange segments
2 green onions, chopped

MIX ALL the ingredients of the first set in a resealable bag. Shake it to coat the chicken, and let it marinate.

Put the coated chicken in the Dutch oven and cook for 30–40 minutes.

Serve it over the rice, garnished with the orange segments and green onions.

PARMESAN CHICKEN

TOOLS
12-inch Dutch oven
7–8 coals below, 14–16 coals above

INGREDIENTS
1 (1-oz.) pkg. dry onion soup mix
1½ cups milk
2 (10.75-oz.) cans cream of mushroom soup
1 cup long grain white rice
1 cube butter
6 boneless, skinless chicken breasts
¼ cup grated Parmesan cheese
salt
pepper

MIX THE onion soup mix, milk, cream of mushroom soup, and rice in a bowl.

Lay chicken breasts in the Dutch oven, with a pad of butter on each one. Pour the soup mix over all of the chicken breasts. Top it with the Parmesan cheese and some salt and pepper.

Put it on the coals and bake it for 30–40 minutes.

PREPREPARED CHICKEN

A lot of recipes, all over the world, call for pulled or shredded chicken. Here are some of them, along with instructions to make the basic chicken in the first place.

Now, you don't have to cook the initial chicken in a Dutch oven. In some ways, it's pretty inconvenient. You could just cook it in your slow cooker or a good stock pot.

But this *is* a Dutch oven cookbook, so I suppose we should do it in a Dutch oven, shouldn't we?

TOOLS
14-inch Dutch oven
20 coals below, 10–15 coals above

INGREDIENTS
3 whole roasting chickens, or about 10 lbs. of mixed chicken parts with bones
lots of water
3 Tbsp. parsley flakes
4–5 carrots, chopped
4–5 stalks celery, chopped
2–3 large onions, chopped
3 Tbsp. salt
2 Tbsp. pepper
1 Tbsp. basil

PUT EVERYTHING into a 14-inch Dutch oven. Put it on the coals and simmer for about 2 hours.

When the chicken is cooked and falling off the bones, bring it in and take the chickens out of the Dutch oven to cool.

While it's cooling, strain the liquid for stock. You can also put the veggies in baggies and freeze them.

Pull all the meat off the bones and put it all in baggies. This can be used immediately or frozen.

CHICKEN CASSEROLE

TOOLS
12-inch Dutch oven
20+ coals below

INGREDIENTS
½ cup butter
1 cup chopped celery
¼ lb. fresh mushrooms
½ cup flour

2 cups chicken broth
2 cups shredded chicken
1 cup milk
1 Tbsp. parsley
¼ cup pimento

PUT THE Dutch oven on the coals and melt the butter. Sauté the celery and mushrooms, and when those are done, add the flour.

Add the chicken broth and the other ingredients and cook, stirring frequently.

Serve it all over rice, sprinkled with slivered almonds or some other garnish.

CHICKEN ENCHILADAS

TOOLS
12-inch Dutch oven
7–8 coals below, 14–16 coals above

INGREDIENTS
1 can cream of mushroom soup
1 can cream of chicken soup
1 cup chicken broth
1 can green chilis
2 cups shredded chicken
chili powder, salt, pepper, cilantro, lemon juice, as preferred to taste

flour tortillas
grated cheese (cheddar or white mexican)

START OFF by mixing the first set of ingredients in a bowl.

Put a bit of the mixture in a line down the middle of a flour tortilla, roll it up, and put it into the Dutch oven. If you place it right, it won't unroll.

Pour on any remaining chicken mix and cover it up with the cheese. Bake it for 30–40 minutes.

CHICKEN SALAD (HOT OR COLD)

INGREDIENTS
2 cups chicken
2 cups chopped celery

1 cup sliced almonds
1 Tbsp. minced onions
2 Tbsp. lemon juice
1 tsp. salt
1¼ cup mayonnaise
4 hard-boiled eggs, chopped

FOR A cold dish, mix all of the ingredients and serve on sandwiches or in flour tortillas.

FOR A hot dish, mix all of the ingredients, pour into a 10-inch Dutch oven, and layer on grated cheese. Bake it (6–7 coals below, 12 coals above) for 20 minutes, or until it heats up.

CHAPTER 4
HAM/PORK

HONEY MUSTARD HAM
THE BEST DUTCH OVEN HAM EVER

Okay, well, at least it was the best Dutch oven ham that I had ever made. Up to that point, anyway . . .

I had tried this one before, but there was a lot of liquid in the ham, and putting the glaze on too early and mixing it too runny made it all end up at the bottom of the Dutch oven. It tasted great, but it wasn't quite what I was looking for.

This time, I mixed the glaze to be more, well, glaze-y—more like a thick sauce or almost a paste. Another thing I did was let the ham cook a little bit to open up the slits I had carved in the top. That way, when I put the glaze on, it would stay more in the meat, and not so much on the bottom of the Dutch oven.

I also cooked it a bit hotter. This was primarily because it was cold out, but I think that it browned and crisped the top much better.

Anyway, here it is.

TOOLS
12-inch, shallow Dutch oven
14–15 coals above, 14–15 coals below

INGREDIENTS
1 bone-in ham
quite a few whole cloves
¼ cup soy sauce
about ⅓ cup mustard
about ½ cup honey
liberal shakes of grated Parmesan cheese, coarse ground black pepper, celery salt, and
    chopped, dried parsley

FIRST, I opened up the thawed ham and put it in the clean sink to drain for a bit. I wanted it to have some moisture, but not end up with a soup at the bottom of the pot. Remember that a Dutch oven's heavy lid will trap all of that liquid.

I fired up some coals and let them get white and hot. While that was catching on, I put the ham in the Dutch oven and checked to see that I would be able to get the lid to close. I sliced the diagonal cuts across the top, about a half inch deep, and put the cloves into the slices.

Once the coals were ready, I put the ham on. Since it was cold outside that day, it took quite a while for the oven to get warmed up and begin cooking the ham. I let that cook for a while, maybe 45 minutes to an hour.

Mixing the sauce was the next step, and a bit tricky. I started with the soy sauce and kept adding mustard and honey and stirring it until it was thick. I went much heavier on the honey, but I was also pretty liberal with the mustard. The amounts shown here are approximate. Then, I added the spices. The Parmesan also helped thicken it a little. All along the way, I kept tasting it to make sure that it was getting the balances that I wanted. I was looking for tang from the soy sauce and the mustard, and sweet from the honey.

Once the slices on the top of the ham started to open up, I poured on a big part of the sauce. Then, every 20 minutes or so, I'd open it up, scoop some sauce up, and pour it back over the meat. I would also add some from the original mix. I could see it stayed on a lot better than the previous time, and it really seeped into the slices.

I'll bet it cooked for 1½–2 hours.

On that particular day, while the ham was cooking, I made some creamy potatoes and peas (found on page 125) and some croissants from a can. Hey, it can't all be from scratch, you know. It was a great meal. The peas and potatoes were great, but the ham was the star. Wow!

ORANGE HAM

Thanksgiving has its turkeys. Memorial Day and the 4th of July have hamburgers and franks. Halloween has pumpkins. One of my favorites of all, however, is the Easter ham. I have no idea why we associate these foods with these holidays. But, there it is. Why fight it, ya know? Just embrace it!

On Easter Sunday, we always have lots of family and friends over, so that usually means I cook. Traditionally I do a big ham in the 14-inch Dutch oven. One year, I did a Dr Pepper–basted ham with all kinds of fruit and veggies in it for flavoring. It was great.

This particular year I did it a little different. It was kind of an experiment. I used the recipe below for the baste/glaze/sauce. It worked out wonderfully!

TOOLS
14-inch, deep Dutch oven
17–18 coals each, above and below.

INGREDIENTS
10- to 11-lb. bone-in ham
whole cloves

1 cup brown sugar
2 Tbsp. mustard seeds (or dry mustard)
1 Tbsp. allspice
salt
black pepper

zest from 1 orange
slices from 1 orange
juice from 4 oranges

FIRST OF all, I put the ham in the Dutch oven. I had to slice a bit off here or there to make it fit. I slit diagonal cuts in the top of the ham. That helps the baste and the glaze seep down into the ham more. The cloves I stuck in the slots. Then I mixed all the remaining ingredients from the second set of the list and rubbed those over the ham.

Then I sliced up the orange that I had zested and laid those slices on top of the sugar/spice mix on the ham. You might want to anchor those orange slices with toothpicks, because they kept falling off the ham in cooking.

I put it on the coals and let it cook for about 3 hours. Make sure you keep your coals fresh and hot. I stuck in a meat thermometer and every so often would lift it and check. The target was 160 degrees. When you get there, you're good! They say you can call a precooked ham good at an internal temperature of 140 degrees.

Finally, about an hour before "done," I juiced up a bunch of oranges and poured that on top of the meat. I poured it slowly, more like sprinkling it, because I found that if you pour it quickly, you wash all that sugar and spice off the ham, and you have more work basting the meat!

I also made au gratin potatoes and rolls (this time I dusted them with salad seasoning, garlic powder, and parmesan cheese. They were yummy, even with jam!

Happy Easter!

This recipe also inspired the next one.

WASSAIL HAM

For a long time, it was a Christmas tradition of mine to make some wassail and take it to work. That really doesn't work out very well at every job, however, so I haven't done it in a couple of years. Still, I like the flavors and the aroma of cinnamon, apple, and orange.

So, when Jodi said that her stepdad was coming over for dinner on Christmas Eve and that he'd bought us a ham to cook up, I started thinking about what I could do with it. She suggested something with the oranges we have. I thought about that Easter ham, and that triggered the idea: I could do the wassail on the ham!

The two recipes are similar but still distinct, and there are some differences in the process and the resulting flavor. So, give them both a try and see which one you like best!

TOOLS
14-inch Dutch oven
8–9 coals below, 16–18 coals above

INGREDIENTS
1 ham
1 orange, sliced
cloves

½ can orange juice concentrate
½ can apple juice concentrate
½ cup honey
1–2 tsp. cinnamon, to taste
zest of 1 orange

FIRST OF all, this was a presliced ham, so it was easy to put the cloves in the slots of the slices. If it hadn't been presliced, I would have cut the traditional diamond-angle slashes in the top and inserted the cloves into those cuts.

I put the ham into the Dutch oven, for starters. I sliced up an orange into thin rings and laid those on top of the ham. The ones that were on more sloped sides, I secured with half a toothpick.

With that little bit of preparation, I put the oven on the coals, listed above. If I could have found my small oven thermometer, I would have put that in the bottom of the Dutch oven to monitor the surrounding air temperature. I was shooting for a low-temperature, slow cook. I still think that in most conditions, those coal counts will be pretty accurate. It was cold out that day, so that might have thrown off my estimates.

After about an hour, I made the glaze from the second set of ingredients. I put them all in an 8-inch Dutch oven and put that on some coals so that it would reduce. I let it simmer quite a while, and then I poured it over the ham.

From then on, I would check the internal temperature of the ham every half hour to 45 minutes or so, and, with a basting syringe, reapply the glaze. It took 2–3 hours, total. This ham was precooked, so I brought it up to 140 degrees. It didn't turn out dry, so I was pleased.

It was delicious, and it captured that wassail flavor.

I think next time I'll go a little heavier on the cinnamon and watch the heat on the oven better to keep it closer to a constant 250–300 degrees.

HONEY SPICY HAM

I don' t remember the occasion that I made this ham for. I think we had family coming over, or maybe we just wanted a special meal. Whatever it was, I wasn't sure what to do. The centerpiece of the meal was to be a Dutch oven ham, but I didn't know quite how to do it. I thought that it should be done pretty simply, with just a few ingredients. I was thinking of a honey and brown sugar glaze. I'd seen a lot of recipes that used this particular approach, but I wanted to take it in a slightly different direction.

At first, I thought I'd flavor it up a bit with maybe some apple juice or dried apples, with cinnamon and nutmeg. But then I decided that was going to be too obvious, and I should shake things up a bit. So I ended up going with a chili powder in the mix.

The idea kinda surprised me too.

In the end, that worked really well, because there was this three-layered flavor thing happening. When you bit into it, especially a cut with a glazed edge, you got the sweet, sweet sugar first and then, a few moments later, a bit of heat. Finally, the salt of the meat itself came through.

Yummmmmmy.

TOOLS
12- or 14-inch, deep Dutch oven, depending on the size of your ham
12-inch: 24–28 coals, split evenly between above and below
14-inch: 30–34 coals, split evenly between above and below

INGREDIENTS
2 cups brown sugar
2 Tbsp. salt
1+ Tbsp. pepper
1–2 tsp. chili powder
1 uncooked ham, thawed
3–6 oz. honey

That's it, really. Not much to it, is there? I kept thinking, "Wait, this is too simple. What else should I put in there?" But I couldn't think of anything else that it needed or that would really enhance it. Simple is good, it seems, especially in ham recipes.

I STARTED off making the rub. This is also simple. I just mixed the ingredients in a small bowl and stirred them together with a fork. Now, your chili powder may be weaker or stronger than mine, so taste the whole mix and see how it balances. Then you can adjust the pepper and the chili so it's there, but not too strong.

You can also choose what kind of chili powder you like best. This time, I used regular packaged chili powder, but I've also used cayenne, and even some homemade serrano chili powder. Use what you like and adjust it to taste.

How much of this you use is going to depend a lot on the size of your ham. I actually ended up doubling this one because I was baking a 10-pound ham. Use these same approximate proportions and make it to your taste.

Put the ham in the Dutch oven and make sure that you can close the lid over it. Depending on the size and shape, you might have to position it differently, or, as I did, cut a chunk off. I have honey in one of those squeeze bottles, so I drizzled it all over the ham. Using a basting brush, I spread it around, especially on the sides.

Then I took the rub and smeared it all over the ham, letting it adhere to the sides with the honey. I let that sit for 10–20 minutes and absorb into the meat a bit.

While that was sitting and seasoning, I lit up the coals. I put the Dutch oven on the coals, and from that point on, it was simply a matter of managing the heat and occasionally using a baster to pick up the juicy syrup and respread it onto the ham. I also had some sugar mix left over, so after a couple of hours, I dusted that back on top for some more glazing.

Since this was not a precooked ham, I cooked it for about three hours total, to an internal temperature of 160 degrees or so. At that point, I took it off the coals and brought it in to the table. By the time we were all gathered, it had risen up to about 170.

My family pronounced this Dutch oven ham recipe delicious! In retrospect, even though I thought the other ham was the best one *ever*, I think this one is my favorite!

DUTCH OVEN BBQ PORK RIBS

A while ago, we bought a rack of ribs. I suppose we were planning to just throw it on the grill. But one day, I got to thinking that it would be fun to try to do them up in the Dutch oven.

I found a bunch of recipes that made it out to be truly the ultimate in easy, basic Dutching. One, in fact, was the purest of simple. It said to cut apart the ribs, put them in the Dutch oven, pour barbecue sauce over them, and then cook them for about an hour and a half.

It doesn't get much more basic than that!

So, even though I like it simple, I can't leave it at that. You know me! So I just had to tweak it up a bit. First a spice rub, then some homemade barbecue sauce.

It is still very simple—only two steps. My son proclaimed them the best ribs he's ever eaten. I was even a little bit impressed, myself! I based the recipe off of one I got from the book of recipes from the 2008 IDOS World Championship Cook-Off.[1] So it's at least got a great pedigree.

TOOLS
12-inch Dutch oven
8–9 coals below, 17–18 above

INGREDIENTS
2- to 3-lb. rack pork ribs
1 medium onion

The Spice Rub
1 Tbsp. garlic powder
½ Tbsp. paprika
½ Tbsp. salt
½ Tbsp. black pepper
1 tsp. cumin
1 tsp. chili powder

The Barbecue Sauce
1 (18-oz.) jar apricot preserves
2 (8-oz.) cans tomato sauce
½ cup mustard
½ cup molasses
2 Tbsp. red wine vinegar
½ cup brown sugar
1–2 Tbsp. crushed red peppers
¼ cup lemon juice

I STARTED by lighting up about 35 coals or so, enough for the pot and a few extra for the side fire. While those were getting warmed up, I got the ribs ready.

First, I mixed up the spices in the rub. Next, I put a little oil in the bottom of the pot. Then I sliced up the onion and layered it over the bottom of the Dutch oven. I cut the rack of ribs into three pieces (you could cut it into individual rib bones if you want) and coated them on both sides with the spice rub, placing them into the Dutch oven. I put that on the coals.

While that was cooking, I mixed up the sauce. I just put all the ingredients into a bowl and mixed it up.

After about a half hour, I added some more fresh coals into the side fire. Within 15 minutes, the original coals had pretty much died down, and I replaced them with the newer coals. I checked the ribs, and they were cooking up nicely.

Pretty soon after replenishing the coals, I brought out the barbecue sauce and poured it over each rib piece. I turned each one over and smothered the other side as well.

I wanted the sauce to glaze onto the meat, so for the last half hour of cooking, I wedged one side of the lid open a little bit so the moisture could escape. Since some heat would be escaping too, I added quite a few extra coals on the top.

The total cooking time was 1½–2 hours. Probably closer to 2. When I brought it in, it was covered with a delicious glaze, and the smell of the sauce permeated the house. Wow. It was *great*!

NOTE

1. From Scott and David Clawson, 2007 IDOS World Champions, with Jared Cahoon.

DUTCH OVEN PORK ROAST WITH PINEAPPLE AND APRICOT

Picture the sharp-dressed waiter saying:

"It's a delectable blend of classic and contemporary, of sweet and savory. A pork roast, smothered in a rich sauce of sweet pineapple and tart apricot and kissed with ginger and mustard, served on a bed of creamy potatoes . . ."

"Oooh! I'll have that!"

"An excellent choice, madam."

Really, this dish did turn out excellent, even extravagant, but it was truly simple.

TOOLS
12-inch Dutch oven
12 coals below, 14 coals above

INGREDIENTS
1 2- to 3-lb. pork roast, thawed
1 (15-oz.) can pineapple chunks, with juice
1 (18-oz.) bottle apricot or pineapple/apricot preserves
1 handful dried apricots, chopped
1 medium onion, diced
2 Tbsp. vinegar (preferably cider)
1 tsp. powdered mustard or mustard seed
2 tsp. minced ginger
salt
pepper

I STARTED the coals and got the Dutch oven ready next to my cutting board. The roast went in the middle. Everything else just got added on top and around it. It's really that easy.

No, really.

I put it out on the coals, and about every half hour or so, I'd scoop up some sauce and pour it over the meat. I roasted it until it was about 160 degrees inside. Then I brought it in and let it rest a bit. While that was happening, I made up some mashed potatoes. I even made some celery fan garnish, just for show.

Fancy meal, no fuss. It just doesn't get any better, does it?

ADDITIONAL FAMILY RECIPES

HAWAIIAN PORK ROAST

TOOLS
12-inch Dutch oven
8–9 coals below, 16–18 coals above
8-inch Dutch oven for sauce
12–15 coals below

INGREDIENTS
3-lb. boneless pork loin or sirloin roast, rolled and tied
6 whole cloves
onions, quartered (if desired)
½ tsp. nutmeg
¼ tsp. paprika
¼ cup ketchup
2 Tbsp. orange juice
2 Tbsp. honey
2 Tbsp. soy sauce
½ tsp. Kitchen Bouquet (Google it—it's a sauce that thickens and browns)

¼ cup orange juice
juice of 1 lemon

HEAT UP the Dutch oven and brown each side of the roast. Stud the meat with cloves.

Put the roast in the Dutch oven on a meat trivet or a layer of quartered onions. This will raise the meat off the bottom, getting it up above all the juices.

Sprinkle the top with nutmeg and paprika. Stir the ketchup, orange juice, honey, soy sauce, and Kitchen Bouquet together. Pour that mix over the roast. Cover it up, put it on the coals, and cook it to 170 degrees.

Toward the end of the cooking time, add the additional orange juice and lemon juice to an 8-inch Dutch oven and heat them up. Add in any juices from under the pork roast too. Let that simmer and reduce. If necessary, you can thicken it with 1½ tablespoons of cornstarch whisked in water.

When it's all done, slice it and serve it with the fruit juice gravy/sauce poured on top.

BARBECUE SPARERIBS

TOOLS
12-inch Dutch oven

8–9 coals below, 16–18 coals above

INGREDIENTS

2–3 medium onions, sliced
3 Tbsp. margarine

1 cup ketchup
1 cup water
3 Tbsp. brown sugar
2 tsp. mustard
1 tsp. vinegar

3–4 lbs. boneless pork spareribs

START WITH a lot of coals under the Dutch oven. When it's heated up, sauté the onions in the margarine.

Then add in the remaining ingredients in the second set. Finally, add in the meat and stir it all up. Bake it for about 1 hour.

CHAPTER 5
SEAFOOD

WHEN MY two boys were quite young, their grandmother on my wife's side adored them. She would take them out to eat at Red Lobster about once a month. When you asked them what their favorite food was, instead of hearing a typical kid response like "pizza," "ice cream," or "peanut butter pickle sandwiches," they'd loudly exclaim, "shrimp scampi!"

She died of pancreatic cancer not long after all of that. But to this day, I can't have shrimp or pretty much any seafood without thinking of her and the joy she brought to my boys. Even though I've never lived anywhere near an ocean, she's just one of the reasons we all love seafood.

BAKED SALMON & RICE

I've always wanted to learn to cook dishes that carry a lot of "Wow!" factor, in both the look and the taste. I've always wanted to make some things that, when I set it down in front of people, they would really be dazzled. Yes, simple and easy is good. I also want to do fancy!

I guess if you wanted to, you could look at something like that and say that I have a deep-seated need for approval and I should be in therapy. And you probably wouldn't be too far off!

It turns out that this dish is actually very simple. It's a one-step, one-pot meal. It's not really a "dump" meal (where you dump it all in the Dutch oven and cook), however. It's more of a "layered" meal. Still, it's simple to prepare and easy to cook too. And when it's all done and you put it on people's plates, it really wows them.

This, for me, is also a landmark dish. It's one of the first ones I created myself, albeit based on several ideas I'd found elsewhere. I took it to fourth place at the Eagle Mountain Pony Express Days Dutch Oven Cook-off one year. More on that later.

TOOLS

12-inch Dutch oven
8–9 coals below, 16–18 coals above

INGREDIENTS

1½ cups rice
3 cups chicken broth
1 tsp. minced garlic
2 (10.75-oz.) cans cream of anything soup
1 (4-oz.) can tiny shrimp

2 medium onions, sliced
2 stalks celery, sliced
1 (8-oz.) can water chestnuts
chopped parsley
chopped thyme

3–5 good-sized portions of salmon (1 for each person eating)
salt
black pepper (preferably coarse ground, or, better, fresh ground)
butter
2 lemons, sliced

I STARTED by lighting up a bunch of coals. By the time all the food was pre-pared and in the Dutch oven, the coals were white and ready.

This dish is created in the Dutch oven, but it's not dumped in. It's built up in lay-ers. Once it's cooking, you won't want to stir it. The bottom layer is the rice, the broth (you can use water instead), the garlic, the cans of soup, and the shrimp. I mixed those up fairly thoroughly.

That's followed by a layer of the vegetables in the second set of ingredients.

Then I laid the fish on top of the veggies in a circle. I salted and peppered each fish and added a tablespoon's slice of butter on top of that. Finally, I put a slice of lemon on top of each fish. I stuck the lemon slices a few times with a fork to get the juices started.

I put it on the coals and began the cooking.

While it was cooking, I turned the Dutch oven often. I would turn the lid about a quarter turn, then pick up the oven and turn it back the other way a quarter turn. That way, the coals were in different positions relative to the food, and it cooks more evenly. I cooked it for about an hour and only opened the lid a few times. You want to keep the steam in to cook the fish and the rice. While it's cooking, the cells of the lemon burst and the lemon juice runs down with the melted butter onto the fish and into the rice. It's an incredible flavor.

You have to keep heat on it. After 30–40 minutes, the coals will start to burn down, so you'll need to replenish them. About 15 minutes after I put the first batch of coals on the oven, I added fresh coals to the side fire, where there were still a few leftover coals burning.

These coals caught the fresh ones, and once the coals on the Dutch oven were dwindling, the new ones were ready to be added.

Not only is this recipe delicious, but it's also really easy to fix. And it really impresses people!

BLACKENED SALMON ON VEGGIE RICE

PREPARING FOR A COOK—OFF!

This dish was done for a cook-off a few years ago, the year after the previous recipe. The cook-off was for three dishes: a bread, an entrée, and a dessert. Choosing what to cook is always a hard part of competing. You want to choose dishes that you can do well, that present well, and that have a lot of that "wow" factor too. In this case, I finally decided on a braided bread with an orange and brown sugar glaze, a blackened salmon on a bed of rice and veggies, and the paradise cookie recipe (found on page 167) I'd done a while back. Once I'd chosen the dishes, I worked out a schedule to time the completion and presentation of the dishes.

I did a practice run the week before the competition. It all turned out great! The day of the competition, on the other hand, was a disaster of legendary proportions!

Here's the salmon recipe:

FIRST, I started on the spice mix for the salmon and the veggies for the rice.

TOOLS
2 12-inch Dutch ovens
20+ coals beneath each one

INGREDIENTS
1 Tbsp. cumin
1 Tbsp. crushed coriander
1 Tbsp. garlic powder
1 Tbsp. coarse ground black pepper
1 Tbsp. thyme
2 Tbsp. paprika
2 Tbsp. salt
1 tsp. oregano
4–6 thick, fresh salmon fillets

FIRST, I mixed all the spices in a resealable bag. Then I cut the skin away from the salmon fillets and cut the fillets into serving chunks about 2 inches by the width of the fish. I put the fillets into the bag, closed it, and shook it all up to really coat the salmon. Then I pulled the salmon out, shook off the excess spice powder (a very important step), and put them into another bag, letting them sit and absorb the spices for about 1 hour.

Then I started on the rice, chopping up all the veggies.

INGREDIENTS
1 medium onion, sliced
2 Tbsp. minced garlic

¼ lb. smoked sausage, thinly sliced
4 green onions, sliced
2 sweet peppers (I used half each of red, yellow, orange, and green, for variety of color)
1 jalapeno, seeded and sliced
1 cup rice
2 cups chicken stock
zest of 1 lemon
juice of 2 lemons
salt and pepper

ONCE THE veggies were all chopped, I put the onions, garlic, and sausage in a Dutch oven on the coals to brown. Once those were ready, I put in the sweet peppers, jalapenos, green onions, rice, and stock. Then I added the lemon stuff and the seasoning. I covered it and left it on the coals (I transferred a few to the top) for about 20 minutes, until the rice was done.

While the rice was cooking, I did the salmon. I put a lot of coals under a 12-inch oven with a drizzle of oil in the bottom. I let it heat up a lot. I actually put a thermometer in the Dutch oven and heated it up to about 400 degrees. Then I took the salmon fillets, put them into the oil, and let them sizzle (uncovered) for about 2 minutes before I turned them over. The seasoning was good and black, and man, it smelled *great*! After another 2 minutes on the other side, I pulled the Dutch oven off the coals, covered it with the lid, and let the residual heat cook the fish the rest of the way through.

When the bread came out, it was yummy! A bit too done on top, but the glaze tasted wonderful. The cookie was wonderful too. I served it up with whipped cream and chocolate syrup as well as a butter/cinnamon sauce. I served the salmon on a bed of the rice.

It really tasted good. I have to say, though, that these experiences where I'm cooking lots of dishes all at once are really tiring. That, and I find that it's very difficult to pay enough attention to one dish to really make it the best. It can be really challenging.

THOUGHTS ON COMPETITIVE COOKING

It seems like half the cooking shows on TV these days are competitions. Even the cupcakes have wars now. My son loves to watch them all. While I admit that sometimes I can get caught up in the drama of the moment, for the most part, I'm not a big fan. I've been a competitor in Dutch oven cook-offs as well. The two salmon dishes in this chapter were my cook-off recipes, as I competed.

Here are some of my random thoughts on competitive cooking.

THE PEOPLE WHO DO COOK-OFFS ARE REALLY GOOD DUTCH OVEN CHEFS

This is especially true of the World Championship Cook-Off, but all of the competitors I've seen, even at small, local cook-offs, are really good. I've been very impressed.

THE PEOPLE WHO RUN DUTCH OVEN COOK-OFFS WORK REALLY HARD

Organizing and running a cook-off is some seriously hard work. Setting it up, promoting it, getting sponsors and prizes, scheduling the judges, and many other tasks, make it a time-consuming challenge. Usually, it's done for free. My hat's off to these people.

I ALWAYS SEEM TO CHOKE WHEN I COOK COMPETITIVELY

Having said all that, I'm not a big fan of competing, myself, because I don't seem to do well. I can cook under pressure, even under tight time constraints, but for some reason, when I compete, I choke.

A good example is the blackened salmon. I did a practice run the week before, and it was incredible. The timings all came out right, the salmon was to die for, and each of the other dishes was perfect too. Then, the morning of the competition, it all fell apart, and I made mistake after mistake. It was a mess.

FOR SOME, IT BRINGS OUT THEIR "A" GAME

However, I've talked with others, and they say that the pressure makes them cook better. It makes them develop their best recipes and hone their techniques.

DUTCH OVEN COMPETITION IS ALWAYS FRIENDLY

One thing I have seen constantly is how friendly Dutch oven cook-offs are. I don't see the viciousness or the backbiting that are so prevalent in other competitive events. I've seen contestants share tools and ingredients with each other, and they're always swapping stories and recipes in the downtime.

JUDGING APPLES VS. ORANGES IS HARD

One of the challenges with cook-offs has to be the judging. It is challenging to compare dishes against each other. I mean, we're talking apples and oranges, here—literally, in some cases! Is this one a better apple than this one is an orange? What's the basis for comparison? Sometimes, I don't envy the judges their jobs. Judging any kind of creative endeavor is difficult.

It's made particularly difficult by the fact that, as I mentioned before, those who participate in Dutch oven cook-offs tend to be good at it. So, as a result, you have to draw the line between varying dishes that are all top quality. How can you call a winner?

Now, even though I'm not the best performer in competition, I have been in and around quite a few of them. I've noticed a lot of things about the competition, so here's my advice on how to do well at a cook-off:

THE BEST TASTING FOOD DOESN'T ALWAYS WIN

There are a lot of things other than the final product that add up to your final score. First of all, in addition to the tasting, the garnish and presentation is a part of the score. How you present the food can precondition the judges' opinions of your dish.

Also, there are people called "field judges" who score you on your time spent preparing the dishes. If your preparation area looks cluttered, disorganized, or even dirty, you can be marked down. Many people will bring fancy tablecloths and other bits of decor for their preparation areas, and they often get higher scores for that. How you interact with other competitors and with any spectators could be factored into your score as well.

THERE ARE SOME "STANDARD DISHES" THAT TEND TO WIN COOK-OFFS

While variety and innovation are a good thing, they don't tend to win cook-offs. Ribs are very popular, as are roasts of both beef and pork. Stews and chilis don't do as well, because it's a little more difficult to find a great way to present them visually. I also haven't seen chicken dishes win as often. International dishes, like asian cuisines or pastas, don't tend to be popular. Exotic dishes that the judges would be unfamiliar with could also be more challenging.

That doesn't mean that you shouldn't try these. It does, however, mean that you're up against additional stress to prove your dish is great. Make it incredible and make it look great, and it could win out!

PLANNING AND TIMING ARE A BIG DEAL

In a cook-off, all of the chefs will begin cooking at the same time, and all will have a deadline time to turn in their dishes. Some cook-offs stagger the times, so main dishes are presented to the judges and then, a while later, breads, and so on.

In either case, you'll want to plan your cooking so that each dish will be finished, garnished, and ready to present to the judges right when it's due. If you have it finished too early, it won't look as fresh and won't be at the peak of its flavor. If it's done too late, you might have to present an incomplete dish, or might even be disqualified.

So, begin with the end in mind. I created a spreadsheet and planned out each phase of each dish, counting backwards in time from the presentation deadline. That way, at any given moment in the competition, I knew what I needed to be working on.

COOK WITH A FRIEND

One of the biggest mistakes I made in my cook-off experiences is that I cooked alone. First of all, pulling off three dishes in three hours to competition quality is crazy for a single person. Second, having a friend there with you is a lot more fun.

Even with my own difficult experience in cook-offs, I really think that at some point, everyone should do a competition. It's a wonderfully unique experience, and you'll learn a lot about yourself and Dutch oven cooking by doing it. Go into it for the experience, not necessarily for the win, if you have to. Do your best, and have a great time.

DUTCH OVEN YOGURT AND HERB FISH

Our family isn't really much into fishing. My wife loves to do it, but I'm no good at it. See, every time I used to go fishing, nobody caught anything. I don't mean just me. I mean, nobody. Nobody in our group, nobody in our boat, nobody. I started to get this emotional, gut-level complex. I began to think I was cursed.

Except for one time, a few years ago, when the curse was lifted. We went out with some people on their boat, in an annual program that takes handicapped kids out fishing (castforkids.org). That day I caught some, Brendon and Jacob caught some, our friends caught some, *everybody* caught some! And since our friends don't really like to eat fish, I got to bring it all home and cook it.

Now, since I don't usually catch 'em, I sure don't know how to fillet them, so I looked it up on YouTube, that font of all knowledge and wisdom. That helped some, but not really. After literally butchering the first one, I kinda got the hang of it, and the rest turned out pretty well. They were all bass. Most were smallish, with not much meat, but there were a few pretty sizable ones.

I'd found, in a cookbook I have, a recipe for a yogurt and dill sauce for chicken. I thought it would taste good on fish, so I looked at it again and modified it with some additional herbs and then put the whole thing on potatoes. Here it is:

TOOLS
12-inch Dutch oven
8 coals below, 16–17 above in the baking stage

INGREDIENTS
A lot of white fish fillets. I think there were probably about 10 fish we kept, most of which were 10–12 inches before filleting, and a few were as long as 14 inches.

The Sauce
1–2 (6-oz.) tubs plain yogurt
juice from 1 lime
very liberal applications of dill weed, oregano, cilantro, parsley, salt, pepper (coarse ground), and any other herb or spice you want

1 lb. bacon, cut into 1-inch squares
1 medium to large onion, quartered and separated
1 Tbsp. garlic
salt and pepper
2 large potatoes, quartered and sliced

I STARTED by filleting the fish, patting them dry with paper towels, and putting them all in a big mixing bowl. Then, in another bowl, I mixed all of the sauce ingredients. I poured that over the fish and stirred it up to coat them thickly. I put that in the fridge to marinate.

I continued by sautéing the bacon, onion, and garlic until they were all pretty brown. I had the Dutch oven over a lot of coals at the time, probably around 25 or so. I added the salt and pepper, then the potatoes. I stirred it all up to coat the potatoes in the bacon grease. At that point, I pulled the Dutch oven off the coals and set it up for the baking, with the above listed coals on top and below.

Since fish cooks pretty quick, I baked the potatoes for 20–30 minutes before adding the fish on top. That continued baking, and about a half hour later, it was all done.

The yogurt and the herbs on the fish tasted great! Fish and yogurt are not very strong flavors, so make sure that you really let go with the herbs!

STEAMED CRAB WITH SHRIMP AND VEGGIE RICE

When my wife and I first got married, one of the things she fixed for me on our honeymoon was crab with a butter sauce. Ever since then, whenever we eat crab, whether at home or in a restaurant, she and I always wink at each other and remember that time over twenty years ago. It's really a romantic thing for us.

Before that adventure with my new wife, I didn't like crab very much. It seemed like so much work for so little meat. But over the years, my perspective has changed, and now breaking it out of the shells is just part of the fun.

TOOLS

12-inch Dutch oven
8 coals below, 16 above (In moderate weather. However, the day I cooked this, it was freezing, with snow, so I used 12 coals below, 22 above, with windbreaks or a hood.)

INGREDIENTS

2½ cups water or broth/stock (see below)
1¼ cups rice
½ lb. medium to large uncooked shrimp, peeled and deveined
1 medium to large onion
2–3 stalks celery
1 cup sliced fresh mushrooms
2 tsp. minced garlic
1 lemon (or splashes of lemon juice)
shakes of cilantro
shakes of parsley
liberal shakings of coarse ground black pepper
liberal shakings of salt
2–3 lbs. king crab legs, thawed

½ cup butter
1 heaping tsp. minced garlic
½ tsp. prepared Cajun spices
½ tsp. salt

I STARTED by lighting up a lot of coals. I had some trouble getting them lit in the snow, but lighter fluid overcomes all!

I noticed that as the shrimp and the crabs legs had been thawing in plastic bags in my sink, the bags were filled with liquid from the melting ice, and it was thick with juices from the shellfish. It was like a broth, so I drained it into a measuring cup. Not quite enough came out though—only about 1¼ cups—so I filled the remaining space to 2½ cups with water. That went in the bottom of the Dutch oven with the rice. Then I peeled the shrimp (It came from the market deveined—I hate doing that) and arranged those on top.

I sliced up the onion, celery, and mushrooms and layered those in. On top of that I poured or shook on the remaining seasonings (listed in the first set). I prefer to slice lemons and layer those on top, but I had no lemons, so I used lemon juice instead.

Finally, I took a heavy object (I wanted to use a meat tenderizing hammer but could only find my rolling pin) and smacked the crab shells to precrack them a bit. Then I arranged the crab legs on top of it all. The theory was that the cooking rice would steam the crab, and the flavors would penetrate into the crab meat better if there were some cracks in the shells.

I took the Dutch oven out and set it on the coals. Since it was practically a blizzard, it took a long time and some extra coals to get the oven up to boiling or rice cooking temperature. But once it did, it took only 20–25 minutes of actual cooking for the whole thing to be done.

Once I saw that the rice was, indeed, cooking and not freezing, I got out my 8-inch Dutch oven and added all the ingredients of the second set. I put that Dutch oven on top of the 12-inch and added a few coals on top of it. This became the buttery dipping sauce for the crab.

ADDITIONAL FAMILY RECIPES

SHRIMP SCAMPI

This is a variation of that recipe in the restaurant that my kids loved so much. I don't know how accurate it really is, like most knockoff recipes, but it's still really good!

TOOLS
12-inch Dutch oven
7–8 coals below, 14–16 coals above
ramekins

INGREDIENTS
1 lb. shrimp, peeled and deveined
1 cup white wine or white grape juice
½ cup unsalted butter, melted
3 Tbsp. minced garlic
paprika and parsley for topping

PREHEAT THE Dutch oven on the coals.

Place the shrimp in ceramic ramekins. These are small bowls, usually designed for desserts like crème brûlée, but there are lots of uses. You can use any small bowl.

Mix the wine or grape juice, the butter, and the garlic and pour over the shrimp in each ramekin. Sprinkle each one with the paprika and parsley flakes.

Put the ramekins in the preheated Dutch oven and bake them for 10 minutes or so, until the shrimp is red and curled. Serve it right in the ramekin.

SHRIMP CREOLE

TOOLS
12-inch Dutch oven
20 or so coals below

INGREDIENTS
4 Tbsp. butter
1 cup chopped onions
1 cup chopped celery
3 cloves garlic, chopped
½ cup chopped bell pepper
2 Tbsp. flour, with 6 tsp. water
3 Tbsp. chopped parsley
3 bay leaves
1 tsp. salt

¼ tsp. cayenne
2½ cups diced tomatoes
3 cups water
3 lbs. cleaned shrimp

MELT THE butter, and sauté the onions, celery, garlic, and pepper. Add in the flour, and mix it all together. The flour and the butter will make a sort of roux base.

Add the parsley, bay leaves, salt, and cayenne, then the tomatoes. Let all of that blend together for a bit.

Add the water and the shrimp. Cover the pot, and let it simmer for 30 minutes or so. In the meantime, put 2 cups of water and 1 cup of rice in an 8-inch Dutch oven, and cook that up.

When it's all done, serve the shrimp over the rice.

CHAPTER 6

SOUPS AND STEWS

FOR ME, soups are comfort food. They warm me up from the inside, and that makes me feel good. I like my soups flavorful, with big chunks of food. That's why I always prefer to make my own over the weak and thin things that come out of cans.

I want to start out by taking stock. Or should I say, making stock? It's the base of almost all soups, and if you make your own, you can really shape the flavors.

CHICKEN OR POULTRY STOCK

This one's not really a recipe. It's more of a process that I go through whenever I do a roast chicken or turkey recipe. You're always left with this big, hulking skeleton carcass, and what do you do with it? It's still got little chunks of meat on it that you couldn't get off with the carving knife, and you can't just leave it on the table and piece on it all night. It's nice to get just a little bit more out of the bird before it's all thrown away.

Here's what I do.

First, I usually just put it away for the night. If I've been cooking all day, as much fun as that is, I'm not up to cooking more. I'll wrap it up and put it in the fridge.

Then, the next day, I'll put it back in the Dutch oven with about 8 or so cups of water. I'll put that on some coals (usually 15–20), with the lid on, and let it boil. Once the coals start dying down, I'll just replenish them bit by bit, enough to keep it simmering, but it doesn't have to be boiling hard. Today, when I did this, I let it simmer for a couple of hours. Technically, it doesn't have to be done in a Dutch oven. You could do it in a stock pot on your stove or even in your slow cooker. But this *is* a Dutch oven cookbook . . .

Then, when it's all done, I'll bring it in and let it cool just a bit. I'm going to be working with it, and I don't want to burn myself in the process.

Much of the meat will either have boiled off the bones or be so loose that it's pretty easy to pull off with a fork. I clean off as much as I can and scoop out what's in the broth with a slotted spoon. That meat will make a great chicken soup. Or sandwiches. Or enchiladas or chicken salad or anything else you can think of for pulled or shredded chicken.

There are a lot of ways to get the good broth out of the muck. I start by spooning off as much of the floating fat stuff as I can. Then, I get my basting syringe out. I dip the tip down below the level of remaining fat and floating herbs and suck up a tubefull, and empty that through a strainer into a pitcher or some other fairly large container. I keep doing that until I've gotten pretty much all of the clearest liquid out. The remaining fat, slime, and other solids get thrown away with the bones.

I let the container sit a little longer, just to let a little more fat separate out, and do the same game with the baster again. Only this time, I put the broth into a measuring cup and measure 2 cups. I pour that into sandwich-size resealable baggies, which go in my freezer.

Then, it's easy to pull the baggies out. I just check the recipe, and I know that I've got 2 cups in each package.

It's kinda cool to be able to get your own stock when a chicken recipe calls for it or to get the right flavoring to start some other recipe. I like the way it carries with it some of the spices of the chicken recipe that I cooked. It tastes similar to all the other broths, but with a slight bit of character all its own.

MARK'S TOMATO SOUP

Some Dutch oven days, it feels like life, the cosmos, and karma are all three conspiring against you. The coals won't stay lit, the storms rage, the winds rush, and it's just plain tough to cook your food. Then the recipe bombs and you end up with something that is almost, but not quite, totally unlike what you had thought you were cooking. Sometimes, it's still edible. Other times, it's not.

I have cooking days like that.

On the other hand, I have cooking days like this one too:

It was truly the first day of spring. The calendar said that a couple of weeks before was the first day of spring, but this particular weekend was truly the first spring-like weather we'd had that year. Beautiful temperatures, sunny skies, light breezes . . . It was a perfect day to Dutch oven.

Frankly, it was a perfect day to do just about anything outdoors.

For several weeks, I'd been planning this tomato soup. I'd read what looked like a really good recipe, and I'd thought of some things that, in my mind's tastes, would really enhance it. It was to be made from scratch, as I tend to like doing. And by "from scratch," I mean from tomatoes, not from a can.

Well, it all came together. A beautiful day, some magnificent biscuits, and possibly the best soup I've ever tasted. And I decided that since it ended up being very different from the original recipe, I'd claim it as my own!

Man, what a day!

TOOLS
12-inch Dutch oven, with lots of coals underneath to keep the soup boiling, then simmering. Somewhere around 20+.

INGREDIENTS
2 Tbsp. oil or butter
2 medium onions, chopped
2 Tbsp. minced garlic

6–7 medium tomatoes, peeled and chopped
4–5 cups chicken or vegetable stock
3 stalks celery, chopped
5–6 green onions, chopped (include some greens)
1 jalapeno, chopped
2 crumbled bay leaves
liberal shakes (at the start and occasionally in the cooking) of salt, coarse ground pepper, dried parsley, cumin, and any other herb or spice you like

1–3 Tbsp. flour

I STARTED out by firing up a whole bunch of coals. Lots of them. I put the 12-inch oven over 18–20 coals and put in the first set of ingredients. I just let the onions and garlic cook to transparency.

Then, once they were nearly done, I added all the second set of ingredients. I seasoned it at that point, and then again later on. It took quite a while for it to start boiling. I had to keep the lid on, although I didn't actually put any coals on the lid. I just kept it cooking and simmering while I made the biscuits.

The total cook time was somewhere around 2½–3 hours. After about an hour and a half, I could see that the tomatoes had pretty much dissolved. Some of the other veggies were looking pretty frail too. I got a wire whisk and kinda beat it through the mixture to blend it better and chop up any bigger veggie chunks. If I'd had one of those hand blenders I would've used that. You know, the ones with the cranks that spin a couple of blades around.

After that, I let it simmer a while with the lid off. I had thought to cook it down some, but it's not easy to get enough coals under it to keep it boiling without the lid on.

With about a half hour or so to go, I added the flour. I actually added it with a fork, so I could just tap it and sprinkle it into the soup. Then I'd grab the whisk and blend it in. That just thickened it up a bit. Not too much.

And, in a side Dutch oven, I made some biscuits, like those on page 211.

So, tonight's meal was a big success. The biscuits were finally fluffy, and the soup was all "wow" and zesty. Yummmm . . .

And, as I was cooking it, I realized that with only a couple of ingredient changes, it could have been a completely vegetarian meal. If I'd used veggie stock instead of chicken stock, or even just water, and if I'd used something besides milk in the biscuits.

SPLIT—PEA SOUP WITH HAM

I know that every time I cook up a ham roast, which is about 2 or 3 times a year, eventually I'll make a split-pea soup out of the remaining bone and meat. It's just too good to pass up. I can't just throw the bones away, either, until I've extracted every bit of yummy goodness out of them.

I had done split-pea soups many times before. I have a recipe for Dutch Oven Split-Pea soup that's pretty much the same as the first time I did it. It's good, but this time I kicked it up a notch. It must've worked, because even though I cooked up a whole 12-inch Dutch oven's worth of the stuff, there were no leftovers. That's good too, because split-pea soup doesn't usually make great leftovers. It ends up as less of a soup and more of a paste.

I've found, by the way, that when you do these recipes, your final result will vary a little based on the way you cooked your ham. Some of the residual flavors and spices from the ham will carry over into the soup. Personally, I like that. It gives a little variety and character. The same is true if you make your own chicken stock.

TOOLS
12-inch Dutch oven
15–20 coals below

INGREDIENTS
1 Tbsp. olive oil
1 sliced onion
4–5 cloves of garlic, minced
2 stalks celery, chopped
a bit of salt

6 cups water, at least half of which could be chicken stock
1 (1-lb.) bag dried split peas
1 ham bone with lots of meat left on it
1 diced potato

generous shakes of oregano, parsley, and chili powder
salt and coarse ground pepper to taste

I STARTED by lighting up some coals and letting them start to get white. I put about a tablespoon of olive oil in the bottom of my Dutch oven and let that heat up on a layer of coals. I chopped up the veggies while it was all getting going.

Once the oil was hot, I dropped in the onion, garlic, and celery to sauté. Remember, if it's hot enough, they'll sizzle as soon as you drop them in. I stirred them up and salted them a little. The Dutch oven was plenty hot, and pretty soon they were browning.

Once the garlic was brown and the onions were translucent, I poured in the liquid. You can use boxed stock or even bouillon cubes, but I prefer to use my own homemade poultry stock. I keep it frozen in two-cup baggies. I thaw it out in the microwave or in a smaller Dutch oven first. I have been known to just drop the ice blocks of stock in, but that makes it take much longer to cook the soup.

Then I added all of the other set two ingredients and let it come back up to a boil.

Once it was simmering, I started adding in the herbs and the chili powder. I added the chili powder a bit at a time. I'd shake in some, let it simmer for 15 minutes or so, then taste. Add some more, wait, and taste. I wanted it to have an edge, but I didn't want to have a recognizable chili taste. In the end, I prob-ably added a little under a teaspoonful. Season with salt and pepper to taste, but be a little cautious, because the ham will add lots of salty flavor.

It turned out great! We all gathered around our new patio table and had a wonderful outdoor meal.

"THROW IT ALL IN THE DUTCH OVEN" CHILI

I remember several years ago, our church congregation hosted a chili cook-off. It was an informal affair, with everyone bringing a pot or slow cooker of their own family recipe. I was amazed at the variety of dishes people brought. What amazed me most of all was that all of them were called chilis. Tasting all of those dishes really opened my eyes (and my sinuses, in some cases).

See, prior to that, I had been kind of intimidated by the thought of cooking chili. So many people make chili, and they all claim to have the best chili or the most authentic chili, and how could I claim that mine was any better?

Here were twenty or so different versions, with vastly different ingredients. In fact, there was no one ingredient that they all shared. Most had meat, but not all. Most had beans, but not all. Most were spicy and hot, but not all. One even had spaghetti noodles in it. So, what is it that defines a chili? Tomatoes? Chili powder? Even a few didn't have those. I couldn't find the common element that was there in all of them, yet they were all called chilis.

So I realized that night that you can pretty much cook anything you want and call it a chili, as long as it's sort of vaguely brownish red and stew-like in texture. And actually, white chilis aren't even red! No more fear!

Along the way, I've developed a few favorite tricks that make my chili my own. One trick is to add just a little cinnamon—yummy spice that adds some good kick, but a different kind of kick. One that you don't expect.

Another is to add about a ½ cup of corn masa or crushed corn chips toward the end of the cooking. It thickens up the broth with a rich southwest flavor and aroma. I also like lemon juice and cilantro as seasonings in the pot.

Other than that, it's pretty much the same as any other chili. There are a few key ingredients, and the rest of it is just whatever you have on hand or whatever your own creativity strikes.

The bottom line? Don't make my chili, make your own!

TOOLS
12-inch Dutch oven
20+ coals below

MARK'S ESSENTIAL INGREDIENTS
2–3 medium onions
2 Tbsp. garlic
1–2 jalapenos, cored, seeded, and chopped
olive oil
salt
1 lb. meat, usually ground beef or chopped beef (see below)
4–6 cups liquid, either water or stock

2 (14.5-oz.) cans tomatoes with liquid, or 4 large, fresh tomatoes, peeled and chopped
2 (15-oz.) cans beans or 1–2 bags, softened
½ cup corn masa harina or crushed tortilla chips

Other Things You Can Add
2–3 bell peppers (use different colors)
celery
green onions

Possible Flavorings and Seasonings
parsley
cilantro
salt
pepper
cumin
cinnamon
crushed red peppers
lemon juice
Worchesershire sauce
crisped bacon

Possible Sweeteners
brown sugar
barbecue sauce
molasses
honey

HERE'S HOW I make my chilis:

First, I get some coals going. The chili will be simmering for a very long time, so I'll need lots of coals, but I won't need lots at a time.

Well, except at first, because I'll be sautéing. While the coals are heating, I'll chop up the onions, garlic, and any other veggies I want to add, like peppers or celery. I'll get those sautéing in some olive oil with a little salt.

Let's talk about the meat. I've made chilis with all kinds of different meats. Most of the time, I use ground beef, but I've also used chunked-up stew beef. I've used venison, chopped up into bits for stewing. I've used ground turkey. I've seen, but never used, cubed chicken breast. You can do just about anything you wanna. I've never seen a seafood chili, but I guess that's because you'd call it "jambalaya" instead, right?

Once the veggies are browned, then I'll add the meat to the pot and brown it. If it's stew chunks, it doesn't have to be cooked all the way through, but if it's any kind of ground meat, I cook it thoroughly.

Then I'll add the liquid (water or stock). I'll put the tomatoes in at this point too.

Let's talk about the beans next. The most convenient way to add beans to your chili is to just crack open a few cans and pour them in. If you do, you won't need as much liquid, or you can drain the can first. I like to put in a couple of cans, usually of different kinds of beans. I usually like black beans and red kidney beans.

If you use bagged beans, you'll have to soak them several hours or even overnight first, then add them into the chili pot.

At that point, it's just a matter of adding the things I like or that I have on hand at the moment. I'll pick a few ingredients from each list. Myself, I don't usually use sweeteners, but when I do, I kind of prefer the molasses.

When I'm seasoning, especially with hot peppers, powders, or sauces, I like to add something in and let it simmer for five or ten minutes before I taste it. That way it has a little time to blend in. Be bold in your seasonings for the final result, but sneak up on that goal a few shakes at a time. If you get too much of something, you can't take it out. But make sure that your final taste isn't timid, either.

I prefer chili that's been cooking a long, slow time. Maybe that's because I enjoy cooking it long and slow. (Don't bother me, I'm cooking.) I really think it's because it gives the flavors time to blend.

As I mentioned before, add the thickening masa or tortilla chips at the very end, and let that stew for another half hour or so.

Happy Chili-ing!

CHILI BOATS

One dark and rainy day, I wanted to cook something. I don't remember where it came from, but I got this idea: To bake some bread, in kinda small loaves, more like big rolls, and then slice them open, hollow them out, and pour chili into them, like boats, then top it with some fresh veggies, sour cream, and cheese.

It was kind of elaborate, I know, but then, elaborate draws me in and gets me intrigued and excited. The weather was drizzly and daunting, and I wasn't sure that I wanted to fight with it.

In the end, I won the battle with the elements, and the food turned out great. The first batch of bread even cooked, as I fought to figure out how to keep it dry and hot on the back porch. The second batch of bread was cooked on the nice, covered, dry front porch. That's also where I finished cooking the chili.

It did my heart good to see how the back porch bread turned out, because I was so dejected and convinced it was going to flop. But it was nice and done all the way through, with a beautiful golden, slightly crispy crust. This particular bread recipe uses honey too, so it's a bit sweet.

Fortunately, both the making of bread and the cooking of chili have huge gaps in their processes where you can shift your attention from one to the other.

I started out with the bread. I got it all mixed and kneaded and set aside to rise. Then I started on the chili, using essentially the process listed in this chapter.

Once the bread had risen, I shaped it into longer rolls, kinda hoagie size and shape, and put those in the Dutch oven to proof. Soon, those went on the coals to bake. Since I was doing the chili, I didn't have enough 12-inch, shallow Dutch ovens to do all of the bread at once, so I divided it into two batches and put one temporarily in the fridge to kind of slow down the proofing.

As I said, it was tricky trying to keep the drizzling rain off the Dutch ovens on the back porch. I used umbrellas and tarps, but in the end, I decided that the fight was over, and I moved everything to the front porch. I didn't try to move the coals, by the way. I had some already lit in a Dutch oven chimney, so I just carried that around front and set it up all over again with fresh coals. As a result, the second Dutch oven of bread cooked quite a bit faster.

As it was all finishing, I chopped up some fresh veggies for some salsa fresca.

SALSA FRESCA

INGREDIENTS
sweet peppers (I like the look of multicolors.)
1 fresh tomato
1 large onion, preferably red

3–5 green onions
some fresh parsley
1 jalapeno

olive oil and salt
lemon juice

I PUT the first set of ingredients in a bowl with a touch of olive oil and salt. Then I spritzed in some lemon juice. I tossed that around a bit, and it was ready.

When everything was done, I sliced open the bread, hollowed a bit out, and poured on the chili. Then I spooned some of the fresh veggie mix on top and finally smothered it in shredded cheddar and sour cream. Wow! What a tasty treat! It was a full meal too, with meat, veggies, dairy, and bread, all on one plate.

CHEF'S KNIVES—TOOLS OF THE TRADE

A lot of the recipes in this section require you to chop up your veggies and cube your meats. At one point in my progress in learning the art of Dutch oven "cheffery," I started thinking more carefully about the knives I was using. I started to ask myself if it wouldn't be a good idea to get a really good chef's knife, or at least one that was better than what I had. I was a bit nervous about it, though. You can spend a serious chunk of change on a knife. Hundreds of dollars, literally. Would it really make that much of a difference in my daily cooking routine?

I started doing some research.

I talked with my sister and brother-in-law, both experienced chefs whose opinions I trusted. I read articles. I checked out YouTube videos. I took home brochures from cooking stores. I did some serious reading. But still I wasn't sure.

One thing I learned is to not bother asking the help at cooking stores what knives to buy. Either they don't have a clue, so they assume the most expensive one is the best, or they have a vested interest in selling you the most expensive one.

My biggest problem was that, as a completely self-taught beginner, I had absolutely no idea how to tell if a chef's knife was truly better or not. The ones I'd been using were the only ones I knew. At the stores, they'd sometimes let me heft them, but you couldn't really cut anything with them there in the store and see. How's a guy to tell?

Well, from all that research and gathering of information, I learned several things. First, the parts of the knife:

BLADE—The whole metal part that you cut with.

HANDLE—The (usually nonmetal) part you hold onto.

TIP—This is the very sharp, pointy end of the knife, used for detailed cutting and opening up boxes. (Did I say that?)

EDGE—That's the sharp part all along the blade that cuts your food, or your fingers, if you're not careful.

SPINE—The dull part of the blade that's opposite the edge.

BOLSTER—The metal part that joins the handle and the blade.

HEEL—The part of the blade that extends below the handle and the bolster, to the edge.

TANG—The metal extension of the blade that goes through the handle in better quality knives.

Second, I learned that a good chef's knife will pass certain tests.

THE KNUCKLE TEST—If you hold the knife in your hand and put the edge of the blade on the cutting block, as if you're cutting something, the heel and the bolster need to be deep enough that you're not knocking your knuckles on the board.

THE TRIANGLE TEST—The shape of a cross section of the blade should be a triangle. By that, I mean that from the spine of the blade to the cutting edge should be smooth. It shouldn't need a bevel to make it sharp.

THE STIFFNESS TEST—The blade should be pretty stiff and shouldn't bend much, if at all.

THE BALANCE TEST—If you hold the blade horizontally, and balance it on your finger, the balance point should be just about at the bolster, maybe even a bit into the blade.

As I went out shopping to find the chef's knife that matched these criteria, I had to add some additional parameters, like the Budget Test. For me, at that time, It couldn't cost more than forty dollars. That's partly because I still think paying four hundred dollars for a knife is a bit absurd* (especially at my skill level), and partly because our family budget really can't stretch any farther than that, anyway.

Anyway, in the end, after shopping and looking and hoping for three months, I found several good candidates in various stores in my area. I finally chose a knife that fit all of the criteria listed above, and in addition, it looked nice. And it was only twenty dollars for an 8-inch French chef's knife.

Well, I got some good bonuses from my work one day, and I went shopping. I came home with a 6-inch Santuko, an 8-inch chef's knife, and a wood cutting board. All the way home, I was getting more and more excited and more and more nervous. What if they're lousy knives? What if they're dull? What if . . . ? What if . . . ? I finally decided that even at twenty bucks apiece, they were still going to be better than what I'd been using so far.

After getting my kids in bed, I settled into the kitchen to give it a try. I got out some carrots, because I knew that it would be a good test. Carrots are stiff and kinda harder to cut sometimes.

I peeled three or four and set them on the chopping block. I pulled one toward me and got it in position to cut. I positioned my left hand like I'd seen in the YouTube videos and like I'd been practicing over the last few months. I took a deep breath, lifted the blade, and cut the carrot.

It felt like I was cutting air.

It was the most amazing feeling. I made one cut and stood there, dumbfounded. I just stared at the knife and at the carrot. It was sooo coool. I got my left hand back on the carrot and started chopping, making the circular up and down motions with my right. I could hear the clacking of the blade on the wood, but I wasn't feeling resistance. It was smooth and quick, and I was in heaven!

Then I tried it on potatoes! And on tomatoes! And onions! And chicken! I sliced, I diced, I minced, and I tried everything I knew how to do. I ended up making a chicken soup out of everything that fell prey to my new sword—a darn good chicken soup too, if I do say so myself . . .

I am now convinced. A decent chef's knife *does* make a big difference.

About a year later, my friend Andy interviewed me for his outdoor cooking podcast. He asked me what, besides my Dutch ovens, was my most valued tool? Without hesitation, I said that would be my chef's knives. Often I'm reminded of just how good that investment was when I'm at someone else's home and I'm helping them prepare some food, and I have to use their dull, cheap knives. It makes a huge difference, and it's not that much more money. Go and get yourself a better chef's knife!

*My father has a fountain pen he paid four hundred dollars for. Now *that's* absurd.

MAD SKILLZ WIT DA KNIFE

Now that you have a stylin' knife, it's important to know how to use it. Unfortunately, this is one of those things I was talking about earlier, where there's a lot of confusion and contradiction. Everyone, it seems, knows the "right way" to use a chef's knife, and everyone else is doing it all wrong.

Still, after looking at a lot of methods and reading a lot of instructions, I've settled into a way of wielding my own swords that is quick, effective, and safe. I've only seriously cut myself once using this method, and that was because I got slack and didn't hold my hand right.

By the way, it's a good idea to keep your knife sharp. The food will cut better, it's less likely to slip and cut you, and it's a lot faster.

There are three keys to the process: how you hold the knife, how you hold the food, and how you use the two together.

HOW TO HOLD THE KNIFE

Since I'm right-handed, I grip the knife with my right hand on the blade just above the bolster, with my index finger and thumb, like I'm pinching the blade, at the balance point. I wrap the remaining fingers around the handle behind the heel. The blade, then, in cutting position, will point toward the upper left of my cutting area.

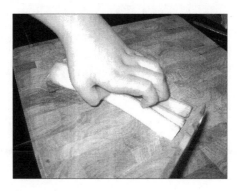

HOW TO HOLD THE FOOD

I use a classic "bear claw" grip. I learned this by holding my hand up and forming a claw shape, like I was a bear. Then I hold that shape and set my fingertips on the food. The fingers curl under, away from the blade. The thumb helps to hold the food in place.

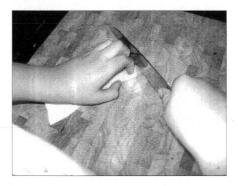

HOW TO PUT THE TWO TOGETHER

The blade of the knife goes up against the knuckles of the left hand. This both guides the cuts and keeps the knife away from your fingertips.

Now, there are two basic cuts that you can do with this setup, and they are the slice and the chop. Let's go through them one at a time.

THE SLICE is pretty simple. It's good for when I need to do a long draw cut, like slicing off some meat, slicing tomatoes, or cutting carrots or celery lengthwise. I put the knife in place above the food, ready to make the cut, with the blade touching the cutting board near the tip, but not high up. I draw the knife toward me, across the food, making the cut. Then I do it again, as necessary.

Although the knife may move down a little bit in the process, it's the sliding motion of the blade that cuts. Don't just press down into the food; that won't work as well.

THE CHOP is a little trickier. It actually begins the same way, with my hands and the knife in the same position. But instead of drawing the knife toward me, I push it forward and down, cutting through the food in the process. When the cut is done, I lift the blade up and draw it back in the same motion. My thumb advances the food and my fingers pull back, and I make the next cut. I continue in this motion, rocking back and forth, my hand moving in a circle, advancing the food, until it's all cut.

The knife blade remains in constant contact with the board, and the blade always touches my knuckles as a guide and protection. With practice, you can get going pretty quickly, and the food will cut in even slices.

Again, remember that it's the sliding motion that cuts, not the downward motion.

There's one more cut that I'd like to describe. Its technical term is **THE MINCE**, but my son and I call it "whonka-ing" because of the sound it makes on the chopping board.

The garlic, parsley, or whatever I'm mincing is on the board, and the blade is in my right hand, slightly raised up in the same position as it is for the slice and the chop. My left hand is over the blade, with the palm on the spine and my fingers extended out, away from the edge of the blade. I rock the knife back and forth over the food, doing a gradual rotation as I go. Then I gather the food back into another pile, rotating it slightly as well, to get a different angle to the blade. I repeat the cut in the same way, until it's minced as evenly as possible.

With these three knife moves, you can do pretty much all you need to make these soups and to prepare veggies for all your dishes. It's kinda fun, actually. It goes quickly and smoothly, if your knife is sharp and you do the moves right.

Really, over time, I've been amazed at how using the right cuts with a quality knife can transform food prep from a dreaded chore into a joy.

(Thanks to Brendon for demonstrating the techniques.)

CHICKEN ENCHILADA SOUP

I'd like to think that I'm an amazing chef and that all the world is in awe of my cast-iron skills. But it's not true. Sometimes it flops, and sometimes it's great, like this particular day one autumn. From the blog:

So much stuff to write about! Good news and bad news.

First the bad news. As is my tradition, I tried to make sweet rolls for conference weekend (see the Breads chapter, page 208). They bombed. Badly. I could *not* get them to rise, and they ended up baking up as inedible bricks. Bleah. I double-checked my recipe, and I'd followed it right. I also checked it against some other recipes in books, and it seemed reasonable to work. So I have no idea why it flopped.

But later that day, I made a chicken enchilada soup, sort of in the style of a famous restaurant. *That* turned out *great*!

Here's the recipe:

TOOLS

12-inch Dutch oven
20+ coals below

INGREDIENTS

½ cup vegetable oil
1 chicken bouillon cube
2 medium onions, diced
2 tsp. minced garlic
1–3 lbs. boneless chicken, cubed or cut into small chunks
1 jalapeno, sliced thin

2 tsp. ground cumin
2 tsp. chili powder
½ tsp. cayenne pepper
a liberal pour lemon juice

2 cups masa harina
1 qt. water

2–3 more qts. water

2–3 tomatoes, chopped
½ lb. processed American cheese, cubed

I STARTED out by putting my 12-inch Dutch oven on a lot of coals, about 20 or so. I put in some oil and let it heat a little, while I gathered, chopped, cut, and prepped all the ingredients in the first list. Once assembled, I dumped them in and started them sautéing in the oil. Once they were nicely browned and sautéed, I added the flavorings in the second set.

The next step is to prep the masa. This is corn masa, the same stuff used to make tamales and things. I mixed the 2 cups with a quart of water and stirred out all the lumps. Actually, I got out my pastry cutter and used that for a while. Once the lumps were out, I added the masa mix to the pot. I was keeping the pot covered this whole time, opening it up only to stir, because it was cold out, and I've found I can keep it hotter inside if I do it that way.

Once that was bubbling, I added more water. I don't really know how much; I just added enough to fill the Dutch oven. Not to the brim, but close. I also wanted it to have the texture of a really thick soup, not a paste.

Finally, I added the tomatoes and the plastic cheese. I really don't like using processed American cheese. I shudder even to type that. My wife insisted that it was the only way it would melt smoothly. Later, a friend of mine said that there was probably enough masa to keep the cheese smooth. I don't know. I just have this aversion to "pasteurized process American cheese food substitute." I mean, how far from cheese can you get?

But in the end, the result was what I was looking for. It tasted great! Someday, I'll try it with real cheese and blog about that.

As it was simmering, I put another 15–20 coals under an upturned Dutch oven lid, and I heated up a stack of flour tortillas. The way I love eating this soup is to scoop it up in a torn tortilla and eat them both.

Now, this recipe makes a *lot* of soup. And it's also *very* filling, so unless you're feeding an army, there will be lots left over for lunches. I've found that when I reheat it, I need to mix in some more water to get it back to the consistency of a soup and not so much of a gel.

BEEF STEW WITH EVERYTHING

This one was all about keeping it simple. It's really just a two-step meal. You brown the meat and sauté some veggies, then add in everything else to stew. Serve it up. You're good to go!

TOOLS
12-inch Dutch oven
18–20 coals below

INGREDIENTS
2 capfuls (or shakes) of oil
1–2 lbs. stew beef
1–2 medium yellow onions, chopped
2 Tbsp. minced garlic
1–2 stalks celery, sliced
2 sweet peppers, chopped (I like to choose a green pepper and one of a different color, like red or yellow. It adds color and a slightly different flavor.)
1 cup sliced mushrooms
2 medium to large potatoes, quartered and sliced
1 large carrot, sliced
2 medium tomatoes, chopped
1 jalapeno, seeded, cored, and sliced
1 (14-oz.) can beef broth
½ Tbsp. crushed bay leaves (or crumble a few whole leaves)
1 Tbsp. parsley
½ Tbsp. thyme
some liberal shakes (maybe ⅙ cup) balsamic vinegar
salt
pepper
2 Tbsp. flour (added at the end)
water

I STARTED by lighting up about 25 or so coals. Once those were whitening, I put a bunch of them under a 12-inch Dutch oven and heated up a tablespoon-ful or so of oil. Then I added the stew meat to brown.

I came back inside and started chopping and slicing veggies. I just added everything into the Dutch oven directly, stirring it up and browning as I went. I started with the onions and garlic, then added the celery, the peppers, and the mushrooms. You can really make this with just about any veggies you happen to have in the fridge. I think the only ones that are "required" are the potatoes and onions. Well, maybe the carrots too.

Then, with all the veggies and the meat in, I poured in the can of broth. Then I added in the seasonings and flavorings. I kept adding salt and pepper to taste throughout the cooking process.

119

It doesn't really matter what order you put things in. It's all going into the same pot, and then it gets added to the heat. Within 15 to 20 minutes of adding the liquid, it was boiling, so I removed a few coals (maybe 4 or so) to reduce the heat a little. I still had some coals going in my side fire, and I would add some to it from the bag from time to time to have hot ones to replenish the ones under the Dutch oven.

Every half hour or so, I'd open it up and stir it. Having that much liquid and cooking mainly from the bottom makes this dish an easy one to learn on, since regulating the heat isn't that tricky. As the coals die down, add new ones from your side fire. The total cooking time was probably 1½–2 hours. My gauge is the potatoes. When they're done, I'm safe, and I cook it a bit longer just for more flavor.

Just at the end, I added the flour (whisked into some water so as to not clump) as a thickener. A roux is also a great thickener. I've also heard that tapioca powder does a good job, and it can be added at the beginning.

CHICKEN SOUP WITH RICE

One spring, at a Dutch oven convention demonstration, my friend Steve shared a space with me, and we cooked together. Among other things, he did this wonderful chicken soup. When I came home, he gave me his recipe. I, of course, couldn't help but tweak it a little to my taste when I made it.

TOOLS
12-inch Dutch oven
15–20 coals below

INGREDIENTS
3 potatoes, cubed
2 carrots, sliced
2 stalks celery, sliced
2–3 cups cubed chicken
1 can tomatoes with liquid
¼ cup rice
1 Tbsp. salt
½ tsp. thyme
¼ tsp. basil
1 bay leaf
⅛ tsp. pepper
8 cups water
¼ cup lemon juice

HERE ARE his instructions:

Put it all in the pot. Put it on the coals and bring it to a boil. This will take a while, and it will be easier covered. Then you'll pull off some coals, just enough to keep it simmering for 45 minutes. With all those veggies and 8 cups of water, you could serve a lot of people with this chicken soup.

When I was a kid, one of my favorite books was a poem by Maurice Sendak called "Chicken Soup With Rice." Each page was a month when you can be "sipping once, sipping twice, sipping chicken soup with rice." No wonder it's comfort food!

ADDITIONAL FAMILY RECIPES

TACO SOUP

TOOLS
12-inch Dutch oven
18–22 coals below

INGREDIENTS
1 medium onion, sliced
1 lb. ground beef
1 (28-oz.) can tomatoes, with liquid
1 (8-oz.) can tomato sauce
2 (15-oz.) cans kidney beans, with liquid
2 (14.5-oz.) cans corn, with liquid
1–2 pkgs. taco seasoning, to taste
juice of 2 limes
tortilla chips
cheese

PUT THE Dutch oven on the coals. Sauté the onions and then brown the meat.

Add the remaining ingredients, allowing them to simmer. Add water as needed. It should be chunky, not runny.

Let it cook for a while, then serve over tortilla chips, with shredded cheese (allowed to melt).

If you don't have taco seasoning or would like to make your own, try this:

1 Tbsp. chili powder
¼ tsp. garlic powder
¼ tsp. onion powder
¼ tsp. crushed red pepper flakes
¼ tsp. dried oregano
½ tsp. paprika
1½ tsp. ground cumin
1 tsp. sea salt
1 tsp. black pepper

MIX IT all in a bowl and use it to your taste. Save whatever's left in a resealable bag or in an empty spice jar.

HEARTY SPORTSMAN'S SOUP

TOOLS
12-inch Dutch oven
18–22 coals below

INGREDIENTS
½ lb. bacon
2 cups ham, cooked and cubed
1 tsp. minced garlic
2 (10-oz.) pkgs. mixed garden vegetables or mixed, diced, and chopped fresh veggies
2 (28-oz.) cans tomatoes
1–2 cups rice
3 cups water
3 cups chicken broth (see above)
salt and pepper to taste
lemon pepper to taste
chopped fresh parsley

PUT YOUR Dutch oven on the coals and fry the bacon until very crispy. Remove all but 2 tablespoons of the drippings and crumble up the bacon.

Add the ham and the garlic to the drippings and sauté until the ham is browned.

Add all the remaining ingredients except the parsley and bring it up to a simmer.

Add the parsley just before serving.

BEEF BARLEY SOUP

TOOLS
12-inch Dutch oven
18–22 coals below

INGREDIENTS
3 Tbsp. oil
1 lb. beef, cubed or cut for stew
1 lb. mushrooms
5 large carrots, chopped
5 stalks celery, chopped
2 large onions, chopped
3–4 cloves garlic, minced
8–10 cups water
¾ cup uncooked pearl barley
salt
pepper
oregano
beef bouillon

PUT THE Dutch oven on the coals. Add the oil, and let it heat. Brown the meat and then sauté the veggies.

Add all the remaining ingredients and simmer until the barley is cooked and the flavors combine.

For a few cool biscuit recipes or to add dumplings to any of these soups, go to page 210 and look at the Basic Master Mix recipes.

CHAPTER 7
SIDES

ON THE BLOG, I usually focus most of my attention on either the main dishes or the breads. I'm not too big on side dishes. Still, they're important, and they can be really, really yummy. Doing them right can dress up a meal and take it over the top, both in flavor and in visual presentation.

CREAMY BABY POTATOES AND PEAS

The first time I made this, I did it in my 12-inch oven. Since I usually make this as a side dish, I'm using the larger Dutch ovens for the main dishes, so the 10-inch is typically the one available. I found the basic recipe for potatoes and peas and then thought it might taste good with the bacon added. It really did add a zip to the whole dish. I found that it turned the milk more tan, but if you're okay with that, it still looks and tastes great.

Sometimes when I make this, we don't have any of the fresh baby potatoes, so I just cut up some regular ones. It still tastes great, but I love it more with the fresh ones. Once again, better ingredients make better results.

TOOLS
10-inch Dutch oven
7 coals below, 12–13 coals above

INGREDIENTS
½ pkg. bacon, cut into 1-inch slices
flour
12 baby potatoes or 5–6 medium potatoes
4 Tbsp. butter
1½ cups milk (I used vitamin D whole milk.)
½ (16-oz.) pkg. frozen peas
pepper

Mrs. Dash or other dried veggie seasoning mix
seasoned salt

I STARTED by lighting up some coals. When they got hot (good bits of white around the edges), I cooked the bacon until it was crispy, then pulled it out of the Dutch oven. Then I mixed the flour into the grease, sirring, until it had a consistency slightly runnier than cookie dough. I let that cook for ten minutes or so, stirring constantly—long enough to bring out the nutty flavors in the flour, but not so long as to turn it brown. This is essentially making a roux. I scooped this out of the Dutch oven and set it aside.

In addition to being a thickener, the flour in the roux gives something for the dairy to bond to so it doesn't curdle and "break."

I put in the potatoes and the butter, letting the butter melt and coat the potatoes. Then I added the milk and the peas. The first time, I was a little nervous about adding the cold peas and the cold milk to the hot oven, but it seemed to come out okay.

I added the pepper and Mrs. Dash to taste (I prefer a pretty liberal amount). I also added the bacon back in. At that point, I just let it slow cook with the lid on, stirring occasionally. In the last 15 to 20 minutes, I added the roux back in, a tablespoon at a time. I stirred it in and let it simmer for a minute to see if it was thick enough. If not, I added a little more.

I've also turned this into a main dish by adding cubed chicken to the party.

AU GRATIN POTATOES

I had actually done au gratins a time or two before, using different recipes and processes, but not all of them have been successful. The first few times, I was un-aware of the problems of cooking with dairy and oil at the same time. Milk, cream, and cheese, when cooked, tend to "break" and clump rather than blend smoothly. There's nothing for it to bind with, and the oils and the milk stuff all separate.

That's where the roux comes in. The flour binds the oils and the dairy together, so it stays smooth and creamy. Even with the roux, you'll want to add the dairy later in the process. If it cooks a long time, it can still break.

As a result, this dish requires a little more attention than most side dishes. But it's worth it to take the extra effort.

TOOLS
12-inch Dutch oven
15–20 coals below during phase 1
12 coals each, below and above, during phase 2

INGREDIENTS

1 lb. bacon
flour to make a roux
1–2 medium onions, diced
3 cloves garlic, minced
celery (if desired)
green bell peppers (if desired)
mushrooms (if desired)
4–5 medium potatoes, quartered and sliced
1 pint cream
1 cup milk
salt
pepper
1–2 handfuls grated cheddar cheese
fresh parsley
a little more cheese

AS AN overview of the steps, the first is to fry some bacon pieces until crispy, then to use the resulting grease to make a roux. Then you sauté some onions and veggies, and finally add the potatoes and the dairy.

The process is actually very similar to what I did for the peas and potatoes before. But this has cheese and some more savory elements.

Here are the details:

First, I took a package of bacon and cut it into 1-inch squares. I got that in a Dutch oven over some hot coals and set it frying. It took a while, because I wanted them to be nicely crispy—crispier, even, than I like it for breakfast.

Once that was done, I pulled out the bacon and also a little bit of the grease. Then I started adding flour, a tablespoon at a time, to the remaining grease in the pot to make a roux. I added it slowly, because I was looking for a particular consistency. I wanted it to be just a little softer than cookie dough. I stirred that to cook it a bit, but not too much. I still wanted a lighter roux. When that was ready, I pulled it out. That was, of course, way more roux than I would need for the dish, but that's okay. It's nice to have extra when you need it. It keeps in the fridge for quite a while.

Then I reheated that extra bit of reserved grease and threw in the onions and the garlic to sauté. If I'd thought of it that day, I might have added celery and some green bell peppers. Maybe some mushrooms too.

Once those were nice and brown, I added in the bacon, the potatoes (which I had been slicing up while everything else was preparing), and then the cream and milk. I added the milk because I was out of cream and still felt like it needed more liquid. You could just use two pints of half-and-half or even two pints of cream, but I think that would be a bit too rich. Then I added the salt and pepper. I was pretty liberal with those too.

I let all that cook for a bit until the potatoes just started to get soft (sort of an al dente feel). Then I opened it up and started adding roux, about a tablespoon at a time. I stirred it in and then continued stirring for a few moments while I watched the consistency change. If you just start dropping it in, you'll probably add too much and it will get too thick. I kept adding it until it felt like a sauce—a thin gravy instead of a milky liquid.

Once the potatoes felt pretty much done, I added the cheese and the parsley. Stir it all in, and it will get nice and gooey. The roux will keep the cheese melty instead of all clumpy and coagulated. The final step is to add another layer of cheese to the top and let it melt. At that point, in fact, you could take it off the coals altogether and let the residual heat in the Dutch oven melt the cheese. Serve it up!

STUFFED MUSHROOMS

One fine spring, I had this idea to try to cook a full seven-course meal entirely in my Dutch ovens. I would invite over friends, and we would all feast. It was partly to challenge myself, partly to show off, and partly just because it was a crazy and absurd idea. I finally decided to just go for it and set a date: the Saturday before Mother's Day, as a tribute to my lovely wife.

I spent the next two months researching and planning the menu. I test cooked the dishes that I had never tried. I experimented. I worked on plating and presentation. I planned out the steps of each dish on a spreadsheet to get the timelines correct.

Finally, the day arrived. I cooked from ten in the morning until the guests arrived at about seven that evening. It wasn't work. It was fun!

In the end, I proved I could do it. It was a huge confidence booster to me.

This dish was the appetizer.

TOOLS
12-inch Dutch oven
20+ coals below for the sausage
8 coals below, 16 above for baking

INGREDIENTS
½ lb. Italian sausage
about 1 lb. fresh mushrooms (not portabello)
Parmesan cheese
1 pkg. cream cheese
grated cheddar cheese

FIRST, I put the sausage in the Dutch oven over the 20 some-odd coals and cooked it, crumbling it as I went. I wanted it in small crumbs, so they'd fit better into the mushrooms.

While that was cooking, I rinsed off the mushrooms and broke the stems out of them. (If you've got enough to be picky, then just do it on the bigger ones and eat the others as you go.) I pulled the cooked sausage off the coals and out of the Dutch oven and let it cool. I cleaned out the Dutch oven but left a thin coat of drippings.

Meanwhile, I chopped up the mushroom stems and mixed that with the sausage, Parmesan, and cream cheese. With a spoon, I filled each mushroom "cup" with the mixture and placed it into the greased Dutch oven. Finally, when they were all in, I sprinkled on a layer of grated cheddar. I put that on the coals listed above for about a half hour.

I served them on small plates and a thin bed of Italian-seasoned bread crumbs made for classy presentation. Good stuff!

SEASONED BAKED POTATOES

The first time I made these, I used them as a side dish for the Jerk Chicken found on page 64.

TOOLS
12-inch Dutch oven
10 coals below, 19–20 coals above

INGREDIENTS
oil
5–6 medium potatoes
sea salt
pepper
garlic powder
dried parsley

I STARTED by putting about a quarter inch of oil in the bottom of a bowl. I coated a whole potato in oil, then sprinkled it with the salt on all sides. I put that in the Dutch oven, then repeated that with all the other potatoes. Then I sprinkled the pepper, garlic, and parsley over all the potatoes and put the Dutch oven on the coals. I baked them until they felt soft to a fork poke. The seasonings took the traditional baked potato to a whole new place. It was great!

FANCY SLICED GARLIC BAKED POTATOES

Here's another way to do up baked potatoes in a way that's not only an amazing taste but a visual treat as well. It will truly impress.

TOOLS
10-inch Dutch oven
7–8 coals below, 14–16 coals above

INGREDIENTS
3–4 potatoes (one per guest)
1–2 garlic cloves per potato
olive oil
salt
pepper
sesame seeds

I STARTED with the potatoes and a really sharp chef's knife. In this process, I sliced the potatoes very thin, as if I were planning to fry the slices, but I didn't cut all the way through the potato. I ended up with a small part on the bottom holding all the upper slices in place. It's tricky because you want enough under there to hold the potato together, but not so much that you can't separate the slices a little. Think the spine of a book.

Then I peeled the garlic cloves and sliced them thin, as well, but all the way through. I wedged a bit of garlic into the potato slices about one every third or fourth slice. I gently moved the potatoes into the Dutch oven as I finished them.

I drizzled them all with the olive oil, then seasoned them with salt and pepper. The final touch was the sesame seeds, for visual flair. If you can get both white and black sesame seeds, that looks even more striking!

Then I put them on the coals and baked them like any other baked potato. Your guests will be dazzled by the extra effort and the flavor.

ADDITIONAL FAMILY RECIPES

CALABACITAS

TOOLS

10-inch Dutch oven
The boiling: 16–18 coals below
The baking: 6–7 coals below, 12–14 coals above

INGREDIENTS

2 lbs. summer squash
water
1 Tbsp. vegetable oil
1 medium onion, diced
3 tomatoes, diced
1 (8-oz.) can yellow corn
salt
pepper
lemon juice
paprika
1 cup cheddar cheese, grated

DICE THE squash and boil them until they're tender. Then drain off the water and set the squash bits aside.

Put the Dutch oven back on the coals, with the oil, and sauté the onion.

Then add the remaining ingredients except for the cheddar cheese. Put the lid on and set up the coals for baking. Cook for 20–30 minutes and then pull it off the coals.

Add the cheese on top, and recover to let the residual heat melt the cheese. Serve!

BAKED BEANS

TOOLS

10-inch Dutch oven
The bacon/sautéing: 16–18 coals below
The baking: 6–7 coals below, 12–14 coals above

INGREDIENTS

1 lb. bacon
1 large onion
3 (14.5-oz.) cans beans, varying types
½ cup ketchup
1 cup brown sugar
2 Tbsp. Worcestershire sauce
¼ lb. cheddar cheese

CUT THE bacon into small pieces and cook it until it's crispy.

Dice the onion and sauté in the drippings.

Add all the other ingredients (except the cheese) and reset the coals to bake until all the flavors combine (up to an hour). Stir it up occasionally to keep it from burning on the bottom.

When it's done, you can add the cheddar, if you want, and let it melt on top from the residual heat.

CHAPTER 8
SPECIALTY DISHES

SOME DISHES are wonderfully delicious but also wickedly difficult to categorize. They're usually one-pot meals, and kinda quirky. I love making these.

Things that make you go, "Hmmmm . . ." and then "Mmmmmm!"

PIZZARICE!

I first saw this while browsing food blogs. I love to do that. So many ideas, so much to learn. I originally saw this one at the "Round the Chuck Box" blog (roundthe chuckbox.blogspot.com). This guy blogs about a lot of food-related subjects, particularly the culinary specialties of the military. His write-ups have almost recruited me!

This idea just seemed so bizarrely cool that I had to try it. I planned to do it for a long time, but a lot of things got in the way. First, I had a hard time finding the pesto sauce. Then, I was missing this or that ingredient or I didn't have time to cook, and so on.

Finally, I had a chance to do it, and here is my result.

I also shortened the name from "Deep Dish Pizza Rice Entrée" to "Pizzarice." As I always do, I tweaked the recipe a bit too.

TOOLS
8-inch Dutch oven
10–12 coals below
10-inch Dutch oven
15–17 coals below, then
7 coals below, 13–15 above, once the baking begins

INGREDIENTS

8 oz. Italian sausage
2 cloves garlic, minced
1 cup chopped onion
1½ cups long-grain rice
2½–3 cups chicken broth
½ cup sun-dried tomato pesto
4 oz. pepperoni slices, cut into quarters
1 tsp. dried oregano
1½ cups shredded mozzarella cheese
some more ordinary round pepperoni slices

I STARTED by arranging a lot of briquettes under my 10-inch oven and a little less under my 8-inch. In the 8-inch oven, I put 2½ cups of water, to heat or boil and dissolve a couple of chicken bouillon cubes into.

In the 10-inch oven, I crumbled the sausage and started cooking it. I like to use mild or medium sausage. I like hot sausage by itself, but in dishes, I've found that hot tends to overpower the rest of the flavors, and all you taste is sausage. In this case, I couldn't find any medium, so I got mild. For Italian recipes, I like Italian sausage better than ordinary pork breakfast sausage. But use whatcha got.

Once the sausage was cooked, I added the garlic and onions and cooked those until they were translucent. You could add peppers if you wanted.

By this time, the water was hot enough to dissolve the bouillon cubes. So I pulled the 8-inch oven off the coals and then added the rice to the 10-inch Dutch oven. I stirred it to coat the rice in sausage grease. Then I added the broth from the 8-inch, the pesto, and the pepperoni chips. The oregano and any other seasonings you want can go in at this point too. Then I stirred it all up.

I set up the coals as mentioned above and put the 10-inch on for about 20 minutes. At that point, the rice was pretty much done. I spread the mozzarella on top. I actually shredded a blend of pizza cheeses, including provolone, Romano, and Parmesan as well as mozzarella. I topped that with some more pepperoni slices, pizza style.

That went back on the coals for another 10–20 minutes to melt and get a good brown on the cheese.

BAKED SPAGHETTI TO DIE FOR

Okay, I know that just sounds wrong. On a lot of levels. But I tell ya, I tried it, and it's possibly the *best* spaghetti I've ever tasted.

It's kinda funny how I got there, though. I found a recipe for Dutch oven spaghetti online somewhere. I don't remember where. However, it called for boiling the spaghetti noodles first, then layering it with the sauce ingredients into a Dutch oven for the final cooking.

But see, I thought about the times I've made lasagna, and I realized that the noodles don't need to be cooked first. The liquid in the sauces, trapped under the heavy lid, cooks the noodles while it's all baking. So why couldn't it do the same for spaghetti noodles, right?

So I got some noodles, and I got some Italian sausage (never make a meat sauce with hamburger), and I came home from church one Sunday, ready to go for it.

But I'd lost the recipe!

I looked through all my notes, all my recipe files in My Documents, and couldn't find it. I did a search of the Dutch Oven Yahoo! group, but that also turned up nothing. I couldn't remember where I'd found it or who'd sent it to me.

So I went out and did a search. I found a recipe on the macscouter.com website. This is a great resource, by the way. Still, I didn't quite like the recipe. It did confirm that I could put in the spaghetti dry, however, so that was cool. But the base of the sauce was tomato soup! Yeesh . . .

So I just started experimenting. I figured that spaghetti sauce was kinda like chili, right? There's so many different recipes, how can you go wrong? I mean, really . . . ?

TOOLS
10-inch Dutch oven
15 coals below, then 10–12 coals each, above and below, once the baking starts

INGREDIENTS
½ lb. Italian sausage
1 medium onion, diced
2–3 Tbsp. minced garlic

½ cup sliced fresh mushrooms
1 stalk celery, sliced
2 (6-oz.) cans tomato paste
3 cups water
2 Tbsp. oregano
1 Tbsp. dried chopped parsley
½ Tbsp. cumin
½ Tbsp. chili powder

½ Tbsp. paprika
1 well-crumpled bay leaf
3–4 Tbsp. grated Parmesan cheese

grated cheddar or mozzarella
feta cheese

I STARTED by cooking the sausage and browning the onion and garlic. I did it over about 15 or so coals. That's all I can really fit under my 10-inch Dutch oven.

While the sausage and veggie stuff was cooking, I mixed everything in the second group of ingredients and stirred it up in a bowl. I have to admit that the amounts I'm mentioning here are approximations. I just put stuff in.

I stirred the sauce mix into the Dutch oven, over the sausage and onions mix. Then I took about a half pound of uncooked spaghetti, broke the noodles in half, and added them on top of the whole thing before setting up the coals as specified above. I marked the start time on my watch.

About 20 minutes later, I opened it up to check and stir. The noodles were getting loose, so they didn't break when I stirred them up. I didn't stir them in when I started the cooking for that reason. I like my noodles longer. I did break them in half, though, to make sure they'd fit into the Dutch oven.

I checked and stirred it about every 20 minutes, with a total cook time of about an hour. This time, the coals lasted pretty well through the whole ordeal. I did have to replenish from the side fire, but not much. The last few times I checked, I fished out a noodle and ate it to see if it was done.

When it was all done, I brought it in and served it right away. Don't want tomatoes eating off the patina of my oven, now, do I? Once it was in my bowl and ready to eat, I sprinkled liberal amounts of grated cheddar and crumbled feta.

Honestly, I don't like to brag (okay, I do), but I think this recipe is the best spaghetti ever!

QUICK FARMER'S MARKET PASTA

Every once in a while, I get to feeling like I'm in a slump or a rut with my Dutch ovening. I always enjoy cooking, but sometimes I just get in this place where all I cook is old recipes. That's good too, because I learn to improve them, but I also want to learn new things and add to my repertoire.

That's why I love cookbooks and Food Network (when they're not doing crazy competitions). One week, I was watching one of their shows. The chef cooked up this pasta with all fresh ingredients, including artichoke hearts and zucchini. He also stepped through the process of cutting open the artichoke. I was enthralled! An ingredient I had never tried, and a new technique!

My son said, "Ew, learning in the summer . . . ?"

So I bought the ingredients and then finally had a chance to make it one day. The results were great! I altered it a bit for the size of the Dutch oven, so it will read different than the original. I also used turkey sausage to make it a bit more low-cal.

This is a great final dish. It's not so simple; there are a number of steps, and you end up with a few extra Dutch ovens to clean up. But it's way, way worth it in the end!

TOOLS
2 12-inch Dutch ovens, 20 coals below
1 10-inch Dutch oven, 15–20 coals below

INGREDIENTS
½ cup extra-virgin olive oil, plus more as needed
3–5 cloves fresh garlic, sliced
3 pints cherry tomatoes
Kosher salt and freshly ground black pepper
1 Tbsp. honey
lemon juice to taste
¾-lb. turkey sausage, mild Italian style
2–3 small zucchini, sliced
2 fresh globe artichokes, trimmed to the hearts and cut into quarters
1 lb. penne pasta

I STARTED out by lighting up a lot of coals. I was going to be cooking in three Dutch ovens, so I'd need a lot. It would all be bottom heat. I put the olive oil in one of the 12-inch Dutch ovens and got it on an even spread of coals.

While that was heating up, I peeled and chopped up the garlic. I tossed the garlic and tomatoes into the Dutch oven to begin sautéing. Now, there's a lot more oil in the Dutch oven than you normally need to sauté, but that will all become a part of the sauce.

I set another 12-inch Dutch oven over some coals, with just a little oil in the bottom, and put in the sausage. With normal sausage, you don't need oil, but this was turkey sausage, which has much less natural fat.

From here on, it's tricky. You'll be multitasking between the Dutch ovens.

The third Dutch oven was the 10-inch, which I filled almost to the top with water. I added a little salt in it too, and I put it on the coals, covered, to boil.

Next, I cut the zucchini into thin slices. When the sausage was well browned, I added in the zucchini, stirring it up.

Then I sliced up the artichokes. It's difficult to describe the process of cutting them. There are YouTube videos that describe the process, but none of them were exactly what Tyler showed. Here are the basic steps:

1. Begin with a full head of artichoke and cut away the top ½ to ⅔. Discard the leaves. Leave the stem in place.

2. Peel away the leaves from the heart that's left on the stem.

3. Turn the heart "face down" on the table and trim down the leaves further with a knife.

4. Use a spoon to dig out the fuzzy core in the middle.

5. Trim it all further, as needed, with a paring knife.

6. Shave the skin off the stem.

7. Cut the heart and stem in quarters and brush them with a sliced lemon to keep them from browning.

So I sliced the artichokes up, cut them into quarters, and added them to the sausage and zucchini. I put the lid on to trap the heat and cook the 'choke a bit quicker.

In the meantime, the tomatoes were pretty well cooked, so I smashed them up and stirred them into the oil. I added the salt, pepper, lemon juice, and honey and stirred it all up. I let it simmer for a while, uncovered.

By this time, the water in the 10-inch was boiling, and I added the pasta.

As the artichoke and the zucchini cooked in one 12-inch, I added the tomato sauce mix from the other 12-inch into it.

Soon the pasta was al dente, the sauce and the veggies all were nicely simmered down, and it was ready to serve! It was yummy! The artichoke was a little wooden, but I think that's because I didn't trim the outer leaves close enough.

This was a great meal to cook, because I learned a few new techniques, and it ended up being quite gourmet!

CALICO CHICKEN

This is a really yummy dish, but I have long wondered why it's called "calico." I looked it up and found that people don't even agree on what makes a cat a calico, genetically speaking. So what's up with the chicken?

Oh, well. It tastes good . . . the chicken, I mean. Not the cat . . .

TOOLS
12-inch Dutch oven
8–9 coals below, 16–18 coals above
10-inch Dutch oven
12 coals below

INGREDIENTS
2 lbs. boneless chicken
1 or 2 eggs
1–2 cups cornflakes, crushed
liberal shakes of seasoned salt, black pepper, and chili powder
cheddar cheese, thinly sliced
a plate or baggie of flour
1 can corn
1 small can diced green chilis
1 can beans
1 can sliced black olives
more salt and pepper
grated cheddar cheese

I STARTED with the chicken, some frozen chicken tenderloins. If you start with full chicken breasts, you'll want to cut them into slices about as long and wide as chicken fingers you buy at McDonald's. I thawed them in some cool water in the sink and gathered the ingredients. Then I lit up 25 or so coals.

I cracked an egg into a bowl and beat it up with a fork. I poured the crushed corn flakes and seasonings onto a plate and mixed them up. All was ready!

Then I put each piece of chicken between two pieces of waxed paper and gently tapped it flat with one of those meat hammers, to ⅛–¼ inch thick. I laid a few thin slices of cheddar over the chicken and rolled it up along the length, then secured it with a toothpick. I took that chicken roll and dredged it in the flour, then covered it in egg in the bowl. Then I coated it in the cornflake mixture. You have to be very thorough to make sure that the seasonings don't settle down to the bottom of the plate. You gotta keep mixing it up.

This went into a greased Dutch oven, along with all of the other pieces (probably 10–15 or so). I put that on about 9 coals, with about 16 or so on top. The chicken browned and cooked in 20–30 minutes.

In the meantime, I opened each can of veggies, drained them, then poured them into a bowl. I mixed them all up and added some salt and pepper to taste. I put the veggies into my 10-inch Dutch oven and put that on about 15 more coals. I cooked those for about 20 minutes, just enough to get hot.

To serve, dish up the veggies in a bowl, put some chicken rolls on top, then sprinkle on some grated cheddar and let it melt.

The family was really impressed! I loved it too.

CREAM CHEESE CHICKEN ROLLS

I just can't figure out the chimney.

A long time ago, I got one of those metal cylinders with the handle on it, and it's supposed to make it so that you can light charcoal and heat it up more quickly. Supposedly, you should be able to put some newspaper underneath, coals on top, and light it. The flames from the paper, they say, ignite the charcoal, and the convection of air through the holes in the bottom carry the heat upward, igniting the rest of the charcoal and getting it good and hot.

Even though that's what's supposed to happen, it's never, ever worked for me.

I've tried all kinds of configurations. Newspaper below, charcoal above was one. Another was newspaper below, then charcoal, then newspaper, then more charcoal . . . Nothing. The paper always burns beautifully. Somehow, it never catches the charcoal. What am I doing wrong? I still use my chimney, but I use lighter fluid too. To the purists out there, I'm sorry. I do it 'cause it works.

I have this signature move, however, with my chimney. When the bottom coals are glowing and the top ones are still black, I pick it up by the handle and do a wrist flick, kind of like the the guys with the skillets on the ovens in restaurants. If you do it right, it rotates the top coals down, the bottom coals up, and then it all heats up evenly. Plus it makes me look cool. Well, as cool as I can, anyway!

This dish is a lot like the last one, in that you're pounding the chicken thin and rolling it up, but it uses different filling, and it's served up differently. The first time I did this one, I made au gratin potatoes to go with it. Good stuff!

TOOLS
8-inch Dutch oven
12-inch Dutch oven
lots of coals—once it really gets cooking in the 12-inch Dutch oven, 8–9 below and
  16–18 or so above

INGREDIENTS
5 boneless, skinless chicken breasts
marinade

The Sauce
1 (8-oz.) pkg. cream cheese
1 cup milk
1 tsp. flour
1 medium onion, finely chopped
1 small can mushrooms
1–2 diced tomatoes
1–2 stalks celery, finely chopped
½ jalapeno, chopped
liberal shakes grated Parmesan

The Coating
some flour
2 eggs, whipped
some crackers, crushed

FIRST OF all, I marinated some boneless, skinless chicken breasts. I did 5. You can really pick up whatever commercial marinade you happen to have. This time, I used a ginger and sesame marinade with some minced garlic and a lot of lemon juice. Italian dressing with some extra seasonings would work great too. I let that marinate for a couple of hours.

Then, in the 8-inch Dutch oven, with 8 coals below and 8 above, I combined the sauce ingredients. I let that simmer until the cream cheese melted.

Then, I took the chicken breasts out of the marinade. I took one and pounded it flat between two sheets of waxed paper. Then I put a couple of spoonfuls of the sauce from the 8-inch Dutch oven and put it in the center of the flattened chicken. I folded it over and secured it with a couple of toothpicks. Then I rolled it in some flour, then the whipped egg, and finally the crushed crackers. These I set in one of my 12-inch, shallow Dutch ovens. I made 4 more rolls the same way.

The Dutch oven went out on the coals for about 45 minutes, baking. I served them up in bowls and poured the rest of the sauce on top. Very yummy!

HOT CHICKEN WINGS

Hot wings, like chilis and spaghetti sauces, have millions of variations. Frankly, I think I like just about all of them, for various reasons. Some I like hot, others mild. Some crispy, some not. Baked, fried, or grilled, it's all good!

I set out to make some delicious hot wings in my black pot, and I morphed a few research recipes into my own variation and procedure.

TOOLS

12-inch Dutch oven
about 20 coals below
8-inch Dutch oven
about 8 coals below

INGREDIENTS

About 2 dozen chicken wings, thawed
flour for dredging
oil for frying
1 cup vinegar
2–4 Tbsp. puréed chipotle chilies in adobo sauce
2–4 Tbsp. chili powder, to taste
2 Tbsp. Dijon mustard
2 tsp. salt
2–4 Tbsp. honey
1 cup unsalted butter, quartered
juice of 1 lime
3 cloves minced garlic
chopped fresh cilantro
1–2 Tbsp. flour

I STARTED the whole adventure by lighting up some coals. Quite a few, actually. While those were going, I went inside and cut up the chicken. The wing tips, of course, I threw away, and the other wing parts I separated and put into a baggie with the flour and shook it all up.

By the time that was done, the coals were getting ready, so I put one 12-inch on and poured in about a layer of oil. I let that heat up on about 20 or so coals.

While that was heating up, I puréed the chipotle chilies and added everything else (except the flour) to my 8-inch Dutch oven. I put that on about 8 coals.

I added about half of the chicken wings to the oil in the 12-inch and started them frying. I fried them with the lid on but no heat on the lid, until the chicken looked done. I could have let them go longer, just to crisp up more, but in the end they crisped up just fine. More on that in a minute.

I turned them once, and when they were done, I pulled them out into a bowl and put in the other half of the wings to cook.

Meanwhile, the sauce was simmering nicely. The butter had melted, but it was looking really thin, and it wasn't blending up nice. I added the flour a sprinkle at a time, and that thickened it, and it also allowed the liquids to bond together better.

The first time I did this, I wasn't sure how it was going to taste, so I kinda went easy on the chilies. I think next time, I won't be so afraid. It didn't turn out hot at all, even though it was a good spicy flavor. Taste along the way and get it to your own particular favorite level of heat.

While the chicken and the sauce were cooking, I also made sure that I had a big supply of fresh coals ready, because that was going to be necessary for my next step.

Once all the chicken was done, I put them all into a bowl and poured the sauce over the pieces. I stirred it up and made sure they were all coated.

Then, for the final step. I poured off the remaining oil in the 12-inch Dutch oven and wiped it down. I put that on a lot of coals. There were still quite a few left burning from the frying, which I arranged in a circle, and then I added a good 5–10 more from the fresh coals. Then I put the chicken, coated with the sauce, into the Dutch oven. I put a small metal grill on top. I put the Dutch oven lid on top of the grill, with 25–30 more coals on top. I was all set for my dry roasting technique.

The idea was that I had all these great chicken wings coated with this sloppy sauce, and I wanted to bake that on like a glaze. If I'd just put the lid on, it would have trapped the moisture, and it wouldn't have glazed right. So I upped the heat and put that metal grill on to lift the lid slightly. That lets the moisture escape.

We served them up with blue cheese dressing. And they were goooood. Again, like I said, I shoulda upped the chili powder a bit. It all comes to knowing just how hot your chilies and your chili powders are, and knowing what you like.

CHAPTER 9

BREAKFAST

EVEN THOUGH I don't camp very much, I think that the best part of the experience is waking up in the chill of predawn, sparking up the fire, and then cooking a hearty breakfast in the Dutch oven. Gradually, the rest of the family wakes up, and soon we're all eating and ready to go off on the day's adventures.

APPLE CINNAMON PANCAKES ON THE LID

If you talk about doing breakfast with a Dutch oven, two things immediately jump to my mind: the Mountain Man Breakfast and Pancakes on the Lid. These two dishes are about as common as cobblers and biscuits in the Dutch oven world. They're both pretty easy too, so you can do it while you're still groggy-headed and haven't had much time for caffeine-laden drinks and waking up.

Here's my take on the pancakes.

TOOLS
12-inch Dutch oven lid, inverted on a trivet
20 coals below, with more in a side fire

INGREDIENTS
oil
3 cups flour
1½ Tbsp. baking powder
1 tsp. salt
3 Tbsp. white sugar
2½ cups milk, with as much as an additional cup to the side
2 eggs
6 Tbsp. butter, melted
1 apple, finely chopped
1–2 tsp. cinnamon
1 tsp. nutmeg

FIRST OF all, I lit up some coals, and when they were getting white, I put about 20 of them under a Dutch oven lid trivet. This is a little metal device like a stand that can hold the lid up by 2–3 inches. The lid should be inverted, with the handle down. Now you can use it like a griddle. I spritzed it with a little bit of oil.

Then I mixed the other ingredients. The dry ingredients went into the bowl first, then the wet, and finally, I chopped the apples and added the spices. How much cinnamon you put in depends on your taste. I like a more edgy flavor, so I put in more.

Then I whisked it all together. I like my pancakes to be a little thinner. I think they cook more evenly. So I make the batter thinner with the extra milk.

Once the lid was well heated, I poured about a cup's worth of batter onto it. I was using my Lodge lid, so it was concave, forming a shallow bowl in the center. Since all of the batter flowed toward the center, I couldn't cook more than one pancake at a time, so I decided to make it a big one.

The idea is to cook it almost all the way on one side, then flip it over for just a few minutes on the second side. If I'd had a second lid stand, I would have gotten two lids going at the same time. As it was, it took quite a while to finish the batter. They sure tasted great, though!

There are many other flavorings you can do instead of the apples and spices too. My wife loves berries, like blueberries and raspberries. We both also love chocolate chips.

MARK'S BISCUITS AND GRAVY

The first time I ever had biscuits and gravy was at a scout camp. Our patrol piled into the mess hall alongside everyone else's patrols one morning, and we were served big bowls full of biscuits. That was cool enough. After the nondenominational "grace" was said, everyone but me started grabbing biscuits, tearing them open and laying them out on their plates. I had some biscuits, but I was wondering where the butter and jam was.

Then they started pouring this white gravy all over them. I'd never heard of this before! But it looked really good. So I joined in, and it was amazing. The best breakfast food I'd ever had.

So one day I wanted to recapture that. I decided to cook a Saturday morning breakfast (Sunday morning is too hectic). It was a little tricky working on both dishes and timing them to be done at about the same time. I also had a little trouble with the biscuits. I need to do more of those to get some good practice.

TOOLS
10-inch Dutch oven
15–18 coals below
12-inch Dutch oven
12 coals below, 24 coals above

INGREDIENTS

The Gravy
½–1 lb. ground breakfast sausage
1 medium onion, chopped
2½ Tbsp. flour
½ cup buttermilk
1½ cups milk
a shake or two of salt, black pepper, celery salt, parsley, cinnamon, and Worcestershire sauce

The Biscuits
oil
2+ cups flour
½ tsp. baking soda
2 tsp. baking powder
2 Tbsp. shortening
1 cup buttermilk

I STARTED out with about 15 coals cooking the sausage in the 10-inch Dutch oven. I also chopped up the onion and added that in to brown.

I also got coals (listed above) on and below an empty, oiled 12-inch Dutch oven. It would need to preheat as much as possible before I put in the biscuits.

While that was working, I started on the biscuits. I mixed the dry ingredients, then added the shortening, cutting it all together with a pastry knife. Then I mixed in the buttermilk and continued cutting with the pastry knife. After it was well mixed, I kneaded it a bit and then rolled it out on a floured countertop. I learned from this and other biscuit experiences, by the way, that you shouldn't work it too much. So "kneading" it was really little more than mixing it by hand in the bowl, and when rolling it out, I'm careful not to beat it to death. Remember that the chemical reaction is already starting to produce CO_2, so you don't want to work all of those bubbles out.

I cut them into small circles with a child's drinking cup and put them on a plate. I carried that out, immediately put them all into the heated Dutch oven, and closed up the lid.

So once the biscuits were in the oven, I mixed the flour into the now-browned sausage and onions in the 10-inch Dutch oven and then added the milks and seasonings. I left that on to heat up and thicken.

The biscuits baked for 15–20 minutes, the gravy thickened, and finally it was time to bring it all in and try it. It was delicious. I knew as I smelled all those spices in the gravy that it was going to be heavenly. I wasn't disappointed.

MOUNTAIN MAN BREAKFAST

A CRY FOR HELP

One day on the blog, I got this kind of panicked email. It was from a lady who'd been volunteered to Dutch oven some breakfast for her husband and friends. With her permission, I'm including it, and the ensuing recipe, here.

It began:

Hello!

If you have the time and energy to help me, I would really appreciate it . . .

First, let me say, that I feel so lucky to have found your blog today. I bookmarked it and will be reading it more often.

Second, I am a NOVICE. Please notice the capital letters. I am soooo inexperienced. So far in a Dutch oven, I have made 3 apple crisps (turned out good), 3 cakes (pretty good), seven-layer dinner twice (the first time okay—the second time with improvements and RAVE reviews), and chicken and rice (never again with rice; I thought it was never going to cook). My cooking experience is with the Girl Scouts, so if I make a mistake, there are always hot dogs and s'mores.

[Note from Mark: Okay, maybe a novice, but from the bits here, not a bare-bones beginner . . .]

But my HUSBAND (you know—the guy I originally bought the Dutch oven for) has GRACIOUSLY volunteered me to cook BREAKFAST in the Dutch oven at tailgating on Saturday morning—for our FRIENDS. (Can you say doghouse?)

SOO, I need a no-fail recipe. I looked at breakfast pizzas, but I'm scared the crescent rolls and eggs won't cook. Can you help?

It was pretty easy for me to reply. I immediately thought of the Mountain Man Breakfast. It's easy and quite impressive. It's one of those Dutch oven traditions, like doing the dump cake cobblers. Everybody's done one at some point.

I replied:

Ah, your story sounds soooo familiar! It took me a while to figure out how to do rice. The most common problem is not enough liquid for the rice to absorb. If the whole thing is too dry, the rice will never cook.

There really is no such thing as a no-fail recipe. There are ones that are difficult to pull off and ones that are easy to pull off, but I have learned from sad experience that even the simplest ones can fail. I must hang my head in shame and admit that even the simple dump cobblers have kicked my sorry butt from time to time.

As far as breakfast goes, I usually don't do breakfasts. I'm not usually up early enough! However, there are a few cool things you can do. One relatively easy one is called the Mountain Man Breakfast. I've done it a time or two, and it's only failed me once (and I know why, and I won't do that again).

TOOLS
12-inch Dutch oven
15–20 coals below, then
8–10 coals below, 16–18 above

INGREDIENTS
1 lb. breakfast meat (bacon, sausage, and so on)
2–3 large potatoes (or frozen hash browns)

Additional Filling Options
onions
green peppers
jalapenos
mushrooms
spinach (frozen or cooked down)
6–8 eggs
1–1½ cups milk
salt
pepper
shredded cheese (cheddar or mozarella)

YOU START by putting some coals (15–20) under your Dutch oven and browning some breakfast meat (sausage, bacon, or some combination of that). You could even cook the meat on your home stove the night before. Then slice or dice some potatoes. Frozen hash browns (shredded or cubed) work well for this too. The one time I messed this recipe up, I shredded the potatoes too early in the process, and they got all brown, and when they cooked they were an ugly black. Yuck. If you use fresh potatoes, cut them right before you cook them.

You can dice some onions and green peppers too, if you like. Mushrooms are also good.

In the bottom of your Dutch oven, create layers. Start with the potatoes on the bottom, then the meats, then the veggies. Season it with salt, pepper, and anything else you like. (Note from Mark: One time that I did this, I also cooked some fresh spinach and added that as a layer to give it a "quiche-ish" taste.)

Finally, whip together the eggs and some milk. Add the salt and pepper to taste. Pour that over the whole mixture. It will soak through all the layers.

Put it on some coals (if you've got a 12-inch oven, put 8–10 coals underneath and 16–18 above (depending on how cold and windy it is outside), and bake it for 30–45 minutes, or until you can poke a fork in it and have it come out clean. Then take it off the coals and sprinkle the top with shredded cheese. Put the lid back on and let the residual heat melt the cheese.

Serve it up!

. . . and I hope the husband gets out of the doghouse soon. Be forgiving. It won't be the last mistake he'll ever make . . .

Mark

BRENDON'S CREPES WITH A BERRY SAUCE

At the annual spring gathering of the International Dutch Oven Society (IDOS), they always have a youth cook-off. For several years in a row, Brendon has gone to cook with me at a booth in the demo area, but one year he wanted to participate in the cook-off. The rules called for a main dish and a dessert. He cooked his famous Baked Ziti for the main dish, but he struggled to decide what he wanted to do for the dessert.

One day (and I swear I don't remember how or where he got this idea), he announced that he wanted to do crepes. At first I was taken back and a bit skeptical, but he persisted, and we looked up recipes. We talked about flavorings and fillings and how to make it "wow" the judges. Finally, he decided on a berry sauce, so we tried it.

We did a couple of practice runs, once in the regular kitchen, in pans, and once on the front porch, in the Dutch ovens. This, by the way, is another recipe where you use the inverted lid of the Dutch oven as a griddle.

In the end, I was convinced. He makes an incredible crepe!

TOOLS
8-inch Dutch oven
15 coals below
12-inch Dutch oven lid
24 coals below

INGREDIENTS

The Crepes
oil spray
3 large eggs
1½ cups milk
1½ cups flour
½ cup water
3 Tbsp. sugar
½ tsp. salt

The Sauce
6 oz. frozen strawberries
6 oz. frozen raspberries
cinnamon to taste
¼–½ cup water
¼–½ cup sugar (to taste)
flour or cornstarch to thicken
fresh mint leaves (most minced, a few set aside for a garnish)

Optional Additional Flavorings
powdered sugar
almonds, chopped or sliced
whipped cream

HERE ARE the instructions, in Brendon's own words:

Add sauce ingredients in an 8- or 10-inch Dutch oven over 10–15 coals. Cover to trap the heat while the berries thaw, then uncover to reduce and thicken.

Put a Dutch oven lid, inverted, on a lid stand over 20–24 coals. Let it preheat, but not too hot. Spray lid with oil spray.

Mix all crepe ingredients, whisk or beat with beater or blender. It should be runny, without clumps. Pour $2/3$–1 cup of batter in the lid, spread with a spatula to $1/8$-inch thickness, and cook for 2–4 minutes. Serve, folded, with the sauce poured on top, with the optional flavorings.

HERE ARE a few more pointers from Dad:

1. Watch the heat. Too much or too little can affect the outcome. Accept that the first few will be tests, while you get the hang of the spreading technique and while you adjust the coals underneath.

2. We used two spatulas. One was a nice wooden one that we used to spread the batter thin. Hold it lightly and drag it over the batter in circles. Let the weight of the spatula do the work. We used a pretty large and wide spatula to lift the cooked crepe off the lid.

3. Separate the finished crepes with waxed paper.

4. With a little practice, you can plate these up with quite a flair, folding the crepes over the whipped cream and then drizzling on the sauce, then a bit of the nuts and a sprinkling of powdered sugar. A little mint leaf or two for a bit of color . . . Mmmmm, you really do eat with your eyes first . . .

5. You can use other fillings, like cubed ham and shredded cheddar, or Nutella or chocolate pudding—whatever you want!

For a few more cool breakfast and sweets recipes, go to page 210 and look at the Basic Master Mix recipes.

ADDITIONAL FAMILY RECIPES

BREAKFAST COBBLER

TOOLS
10-inch Dutch oven
6–7 coals below, 12–14 coals above

INGREDIENTS
4 medium apples, peeled and sliced
¼ cup honey
1 tsp. cinnamon
2 Tbsp. butter, melted
2 cups granola cereal

MIX ALL the ingredients up, put it on the coals, and cook until apples are soft.

GERMAN PANCAKES

My dear wife used to make these a lot more often when we were first married. I love these!

TOOLS
12-inch Dutch oven
10–12 coals below, 20–24 coals above

INGREDIENTS
9 eggs
1½ cups milk
1½ cups flour
¾ tsp. salt
9 Tbsp. butter
lemon juice
powdered sugar

FIRE UP the coals and preheat the Dutch oven.

Whip the eggs until they're thick and lemon colored. Add the milk, flour, and salt. Mix them up.

Melt the butter in the preheated oven, covering the inner base.

Pour in the batter, cover with the lid, and bake for 25–30 minutes.

When you serve it up, spritz it with lemon juice and sprinkle on powdered sugar. Or you can just use butter and maple syrup, like other pancakes.

CHAPTER 10
DESSERTS

I WANT to get really good at Dutch oven desserts. I can do quite a few, but I really need some practice to take it to the next level. If you're doing a fancy meal, a great dessert can really top it off. A lame one can really be a letdown. If that's the case, it's almost better to not have dessert, in my opinion.

DUTCH OVEN COBBLERS AND DUMP CAKES

Ah, the humble cobbler. It almost never fails. Whenever I tell someone I love to cook in Dutch ovens, their eyes get wistful and their countenance becomes almost angelic. Then they say something like, "Oh, I remember once I had the most delicious dessert out of a Dutch oven! It was at a campout (or cookout, or whatever) at (someone's)! It had peaches and cake, and we ate it with ice cream, and it was incredible!"

It doesn't matter how complex and intricate my dishes may be, or how they rate on the gourmet scale, they will never compare to that delicious cobbler that Great-Uncle Wilbur makes with cake mixes and canned peaches!

And I have to admit that I love them too! I love them because they're easy and satisfying! If I'm bustin' my back making the most elaborate of dinners, I can count on a cobbler to finish it off in ease and style.

There are as many variations on this standard dish as there are great-uncles. Here's my version:

THE DUMP CAKE COBBLER

TOOLS
12-inch Dutch oven
12 coals below, 12 coals above

INGREDIENTS
2 (16-oz.) cans peaches
1 (18-oz.) box yellow cake mix
4 Tbsp. butter
¼ cup brown sugar
cinnamon

THE INSTRUCTIONS on this one couldn't be more simple. Start by pouring 1 can of peaches into the Dutch oven, with the juices. Drain the other one and add it in.

Then sprinkle the yellow cake mix on top, covering the peaches as much as possible. Cut up the butter into pats and bits and scatter them on top of the cake mix. Crumble the brown sugar on top, and finally sprinkle on some cinnamon.

Put it out on the coals and let it bake for 35–45 minutes. The liquid will boil up and mix with the cake mix powders. The sugar will melt and caramelize with the butter, and it will all be yummy!

Let it cool a little, but not too much, then serve it up with whipped cream or ice cream.

Dump cake cobblers come in many different varieties and flavors. Here's another one I've done and enjoyed.

BLACK FOREST CHOCOLATE DUMP CAKE

TOOLS
12-inch Dutch oven
12 coals below, 12 coals above

INGREDIENTS
2 (21-oz.) cans cherry pie filling
1 (12-oz.) can non-diet cola (I prefer Dr Pepper)
1 (18-oz.) box chocolate cake mix
a little bit of brown sugar
½ cup chopped pecans
1 cube butter

I STARTED by pouring the 2 cans of cherry pie filling in the bottom of the oven and spreading them around. Then I poured in the can of cola. Pie fillings don't have as much liquid as canned peaches, so you'll need to add more. That's where the cola comes in. It also adds a wonderful flavor. On top of that, I sprinkled and spread that chocolate cake mix.

I sprinkled on a few crumbs of brown sugar and then tossed on the nuts. Finally, I cut the butter into small chunks and spread them over the top.

That's it. Then it goes on the coals and bakes for a while, 30–40 minutes. You want there to be a nice crust on top.

SIMPLE DUTCH OVEN APPLE PIE

I can still remember the first time I attempted to make an apple pie. It was, in fact, the first baked pie I had ever made. EVER. I had no idea what I was up against.

I muddled through the recipe I had found, but halfway through the cooking, my coals went out. I guess they were damp or something. It took me a long time to get more lit up and on the oven. In the meantime, the damage had been done. When the cooking is interrupted like that, it turns everything to mush. My family ate a bit of it anyway, to humor me, but it was pretty pathetic.

A year later, I tried again, and it turned out much better—more like a real pie should be. I've done it several times since then, and it keeps improving each try.

TOOLS
12-inch Dutch oven
10 coals below, 18 coals above

INGREDIENTS

The Crust (I made two batches, each from this ingredient list)
1¼ cups shortening
3 cups flour
1 Tbsp. vinegar
5 Tbsp. water
1 egg
some softened butter

The Filling
6–7 large apples, peeled and sliced
1 cup sugar
1 tsp. cinnamon
a shake or two of nutmeg
2 Tbsp. flour
½ cup chopped nuts (I used almonds.)
¼ cup raisins
½ pint (1 carton) heavy whipping cream
milk

I STARTED out by making the crust. Though I am *not* an expert crust maker by any means, I have learned a few things that make it a little bit better. I poured everything into a bowl and used a pastry cutter to mix it all up. Those are hard on my wrists. But they work.

Then I dumped it onto a couple of sheets of waxed paper, side by side, and layered some more paper on top. Then I rolled it out. I dusted it with flour, folded it over on itself, and rolled it out again. I repeated this process a few times, until I finally folded it up into a tight bundle, put it into a resealable baggie, and put it in the fridge.

Then I did it all over again with the second batch of dough. Believe me, you'll need two batches.

A long time later, when it's time to actually make the pie, I got out the crust dough batches and rolled one of them out into a circle. I used the Dutch oven lid as a pattern to cut out a good circle. This would be the bottom of the pie.

Here's a cool trick to use to place it properly: With the circle cut out, in between two layers of waxed paper, fold it in half. Then peel off the outer layer of waxed paper, so there's sort of a crust "taco" half circle with a folded sheet of waxed paper inside. Then lay that down on one side of the bottom of the Dutch oven. Finally, flip the upper half of the crust over the other half of the Dutch oven and peel off the waxed paper, and your bottom crust is perfectly placed. Since it was cut from the lid, it'll be just a bit too big for the bottom. That's part of the plan. Once it's in place, gently form it into the corner where the base meets the side of the pot.

Then I rolled out some more dough and cut it into strips 2–2½ inches wide, as long as the rolled-out dough would go. I put these strips around the "wall" of the Dutch oven, lightly smooshing it together with the base crust. I kept doing that until I had a nice wall all the way around the Dutch oven. I softened up the butter and smeared that around the inside of the crust. That added to the flavor, and it also helped the crust to not get so soggy with all the liquid in the apples and other filling.

Finally, I rolled out the last batch of dough and cut another circle with the Dutch oven lid. I set that aside, since that would become the pie top.

I decided that this would be a good time to go out and get some coals lit.

Then it was time to make the filling. I peeled and sliced the apples. After cutting the apples away from the cores, I sliced them really thin. I put them and all the other filling ingredients (except the milk) in a bowl and stirred it up. I poured this mixture into the crust.

I picked up the top crust circle and played the same half-circle game to get it placed. Then I cut out some vent slices, shaped like leaves, and used those pieces as decorative bits on the crust top. I sprinkled milk on top of it and then followed with some more cinnamon and sugar over the top crust.

That went on the coals for about an hour or so, and I turned the oven about every 15–20 minutes. Finally it was done!

I love hot apple pie on autumn evenings when it's starting to get a little bit chilly. Amazing!

PUMPKIN PIE

I can remember the first time I ever made a pumpkin pie. One year my wife and I went to a Halloween party with our kids. One of the things we did there was decorate some cool small pumpkins. One of the parents and I got to talking, and I mentioned that it would be fun to make a pumpkin pie in my Dutch oven. Of course, having my tendency to make things more difficult for myself than normal, I decided that I wanted to make it from scratch. I mean, from a pumpkin, not from a can.

After that party, I did a lot of research and talked about it to pretty much anyone who would listen. Anywhere. Anytime. I finally put together what I felt was a good composite recipe. At least, I assumed it was. I mean, after all, if you read it on the Net, it must be true, right?

PART I

THE PUMPKIN AND THE SEEDS

TOOLS
2 12-inch Dutch ovens
16 coals above, 8 coals below
8- or 10-inch Dutch oven
12–15 coals below

INGREDIENTS
2 small pie pumpkins
½ cup water
brown sugar

I BOUGHT a couple of small pie pumpkins. My research showed me that you don't want to make pie from the big jack-o'-lantern pumpkins. The small ones are supposed to be sweeter and a little less stringy. I got the pumpkins, sliced them in quarters, and scraped out the seeds and fibers. I arranged the slices in the bottom of my two 12-inch, shallow Dutch ovens, one full pumpkin in each oven. I poured about ¼ cup of water in each. I used a fork to poke holes in the flesh of the pumpkin slices, then I sprinkled about ¼ cup of brown sugar in the "boat" of each pumpkin slice.

These I put on coals, with 8–9 coals below and 16 or so on top. I baked them for about an hour each, until I could stick them with a fork and have it push through very easily. The holes in the pumpkin flesh helped the melted brown sugar seep in instead of just running off to the bottom of the Dutch oven.

Now, while they were baking, I washed, separated, and dried the seeds. More with them later.

Once the pumpkins were squishy, I pulled them off the coals. I let them cool a bit, then scooped the pumpkin flesh out of the skins and plopped it into a bowl, where I mushed and squashed and stirred it all up. Another time I made this, I used a powered blender to purée it. I have done it with a hand-crank egg beater too. All can work well, but the blender was the easiest of all. Whichever way you do it, make sure that it is well puréed so that you don't get stringy bits in the pie.

I poured in a little more of the sugar syrup from the bottom of one of the Dutch ovens. Then I covered the bowl with plastic and put it in the fridge. It ended up being a bit too much pumpkin, but that left extra for freezing and other dishes.

The seeds, in the meantime, were dry. They dried fast because I put them on a baking sheet and set it in my kitchen oven at about 250 degrees. Yes, I cheated.

I put the seeds in a bowl, with a few tablespoons of olive oil and some liberal shakes of seasoned salt, regular salt, and black pepper. I stirred that up, and then put it into the bottom of an 8- or 10-inch Dutch oven. I put that on top of about 16 or so still-burning coals. Maybe more.

I put the lid on to trap the heat and stirred it every 5–10 minutes. Once they got a darker brown, I pulled them off and let them cool. Delicious! Great for munching with a movie!

PART II

THE PIE

The next day, I made the pumpkin pie. It happened to be a Sunday. In the morning, I made the pie crust dough, like I did for the apple pie. Then, after church, I mixed up the filling, assembled it all, and baked it.

TOOLS
12-inch Dutch oven
18 coals above, 10 coals below

INGREDIENTS
3 cups pumpkin mash
6 eggs, separated
1 cup sugar
2 Tbsp. flour
1 tsp. salt
2 tsp. cinnamon
2 tsp. nutmeg
1 tsp. ground mace
1 (12-oz.) can evaporated milk
1 cup heavy cream

1 tsp. ginger
2 tsp. butter, melted
¼ tsp. ground cloves

THE FIRST thing I did was make the crust (see apple pie recipe for ingredients list and directions) and put that into the 12-inch Dutch oven. That went a lot smoother than the last time I did it (the apple pie). Bit by bit I'm getting pretty good at it!

Some people like to build the pie in a normal pie plate and then put that in the bottom of the Dutch oven. I like just building the crust right in the Dutch oven itself. I spray it with cooking spray first and then just lay it in.

With the crust in place, I set about mixing the filling. I started with the pumpkin I made the other day. I found that I had made way too much pumpkin purée for one pie, so I just measured out 3 generous cups and later froze the remainder.

Next I separated the eggs. The yolks went in with the pumpkin, and the whites I set aside. Everything else went into the mix. It looked a little runny to me at first, but in the final baking, it was perfect.

Then I whipped up the egg whites. I did it by hand, with one of those hand-crank beaters, so that shows you how dumb I am. It took a while, but eventually it got to the point where it was fluffy. They tell me you want to do it until it forms peaks that don't melt right away. Then I folded that into the whole mix.

I poured it all into the crust in the Dutch oven and set it on the coals.

The pie took quite a while to cook—probably about an hour and 20 or 30 minutes. I kept the coals pretty hot, maintaining 350 degrees with the number of coals listed above, plus a few more.

Finally, I could stick a fork in it and pull it out clean. It was odd, because most pumpkin pies I've seen kinda sag in the middle, and this one was humped up. But as it cooled, it settled to flat.

After dinner, we dished it up with the aerosol cans of whipped cream. It was delicious. It was the lightest, fluffiest pumpkin pie I'd ever eaten. I think that might have been because of the whipped egg whites. The spices made the flavor amazing.

COOKIN' IN THE COLD

As winter approaches, many folks will put their Dutch ovens into storage. There are various methods of "winterizing" them, most of them involving making sure they're clean and dry and don't have a lot of oil in the bottom that can go rancid before they get pulled out again in the late spring or early summer. After all, cooking outdoors is for warm weather, right?

At my house, I have a simple method of keeping my Dutch ovens ready for spring: I use them all winter. The herbal roast turkey is now a family Christmas tradition, as is the pumpkin pie for post-Halloween. Another favorite was the Snow Crab Legs cooked in a blizzard.

Let me also state, for the record, that I'm not cooking these dishes "in the wild." Virtually all of my cooking is done on my back porch. As a result, I'm not standing out shivering while my food cooks. I'm inside, snug, usually watching whatever my kids have on the TV. This is not "roughing it" by any stretch of the imagination.

I've found that in winter cooking there are primarily four issues you have to deal with: cold, wind, rain, and snow.

DEALING WITH THE COLD

This is probably the simplest of all issues to adapt to: Simply add more coals. How many? Well, that depends on how cold it is. If you're dealing with general wintry temperatures of, say, between 20 and 40 degrees Fahrenheit, I'd probably start with two extra coals below, and three to four above, in basic baking and roasting. More if it's colder, and less if warmer.

What you're cooking also makes a difference. If you're cooking a stew, then you've got more flexibility, because you can go a bit hotter with less risk of burning. If your heat is too low, you simply cook it longer. However, if you're doing bread, then it's more critical to get the heat right. Too much heat can burn. In that case, I would err on the side of caution and not pile the coals on too high.

DEALING WITH THE WIND

A lot of cooks I know have fancy tables with wind screens, or wind blockers made of sheet metal, in all kinds of configurations. I've got mixed feelings about that. I think that wind, if you understand it and plan for it, can actually be your friend. Wind blowing across the coals feeds them more oxygen, stoking them up, so they actually burn hotter. When it's cold outside, that can be a good thing.

The downside is that it's a little tougher to regulate the temperature, since gusts will come and go. So if you're doing a dish where steady temperature is more critical, like bread, you might want to go with a wind screen or rotate the Dutch oven more frequently, to avoid hot spots.

Also, keep in mind that since the coals are burning hotter, they will also burn faster, so you need to replenish them more often.

A light, steady breeze is adaptable, but a heavier wind can also take a lot of your heat away with it. In those cases, I'd add more coals, like in the cold.

DEALING WITH THE RAIN

There are two basic problems with Dutchin' in the rain. One is that the rain could put out your coals. The other is that if it starts raining pretty hard pretty quickly, the cold rain on the hot Dutch oven could crack or damage it. Either scenario is not pretty.

Generally speaking, if it looks like rain, I'll cook under some shelter. My front porch is covered, so it's still ventilated but I'm not getting rained on. I have set up my Dutch ovens in my garage, but I caution you about that. Charcoal gives off carbon monoxide and could be deadly. My garage is also well ventilated. I can open the big doors in front, and a door in the back, and the winds blow through. I don't know scientifically if it would make a difference, but speaking personally, I wouldn't do Dutch oven in an enclosed space with only one door open. The air has to be able to flow through the space.

My in-laws gave me this big, round, cylindrical metal hood that's supposedly designed to cover Dutch ovens. It works, and I can even stack two 12-inch Dutch ovens under it, but even though there are holes around the lower rim and a vent on top, it doesn't allow enough air circulation. I've had times, trying it out, when it actually extinguished the coals. I don't recommend it.

One quick and easy solution that might work, if there's not too much wind, would be to set up a big patio umbrella over the ovens.

DEALING WITH THE SNOW

Problems with snow are similar to problems with the rain. I've found that, unless it's a freaky, whiteout blizzard, I can continue cooking in flurries or even relatively steady snow. Covering it somehow is a good strategy, like the umbrella or the hood, as long as you can keep air flowing over the coals.

Ultimately, in all of this, even though I'm cooking from the relative comfort of my heated home, I still think from time to time about my pioneer ancestors who had to cook in their Dutch ovens regardless of the weather. If they didn't cook, they didn't eat. So is it possible to make good food in tough weather? Yes. Don't let it stop you!

PARADISE COOKIE WEDGE

Warning: This recipe has been condemned by many heart and health organizations worldwide. It is not recommended for anyone on Weight Watchers, Body-for-LIFE, Atkins, or any other weight loss plan. It *is* delicious, however . . .

The first time I ever did the Mother's Day feast meal, this was the dessert course. That was at my dear wife's request. It didn't take much convincing to make me want to do it!

TOOLS

10-inch Dutch oven
7 coals below, 14 coals above
8-inch Dutch oven
10 coals below

INGREDIENTS

The Cookie Dough
1 cup all-purpose flour
½ tsp. baking soda
¼ tsp. baking powder
½ cup (1 stick) butter, softened
⅓ cup granulated sugar
1 egg
1 Tbsp. milk
½ tsp. vanilla extract
½ cup shredded coconut

The Crust
6 Tbsp. butter
¼ cup sugar
1½ cups graham cracker crumbs
1¼ cups semisweet chocolate chips
½ cup chopped walnuts

The Drizzle
½ cup (1 stick) butter, softened
3 Tbsp. granulated sugar
1½ tsp. cinnamon
vanilla ice cream
chocolate syrup
caramel syrup
more chopped walnuts

I STARTED by combining all the dry ingredients in the first set and set it aside. Then I blended the sugar and butter from the second set together, whipping it as best I could. I added in the other wet ingredients and mixed them all up, then added the dry mix from the first set. That was my basic cookie dough.

I put the 10-inch Dutch oven on the coals and melted the butter with the sugar. While that was melting, I crumbled the graham crackers. Once the butter was melted, I brought it in and added the crumbs, smoothing it all into a crust on the bottom of the Dutch oven. Onto that went a layer of chocolate chips. I would have added the walnuts at that point too, but my wife doesn't like walnuts, so we don't have them in the house.

On top of that, I spread the cookie dough. That all went on the coals and baked for about 35 minutes or so.

When that was nearing completion, I mixed the cinnamon drizzle set of ingredients in my 8-inch Dutch oven and let them all melt together.

It serves best when it's hot. Cut a wedge of the cookie and put it on a plate. Drizzle the cinnamon, the caramel, and the chocolate syrups over it in decorative ways and dollop on the ice cream.

Then call the paramedics . . .

CHOCOLATE CAKE WITH CHOCOLATE PEANUT BUTTER FROSTING

This one's a kind of busy recipe. When I first read it, it called for boiling some of the ingredients before mixing them all together. I'm honestly not sure what purpose it served, but I did it anyway!

It turned out really tasty. It was a rich, yummy chocolate. The frosting was a bit thick and hard to spread the first time, so I upped the milk and the butter in the recipe a little. That made it a bit smoother the next time.

Here it is:

THE CAKE

TOOLS
8-inch Dutch oven
10–12 coals below
12-inch Dutch oven
8 coals below, 16–18 coals above

INGREDIENTS
2 cups sugar
2 cups flour
1 tsp. baking soda

1 cup water
1 cup butter or margarine
¼ cup cocoa

2 eggs, beaten
½ cup sour cream

FIRST, I set some coals on to burn. While those were getting white, I mixed the first set of ingredients in a bowl. Then I put the next set into the 8-inch Dutch oven and put that on some coals. I stirred it frequently and took it off once it was boiling. I poured it into the dry ingredients gradually, while stirring. Then I added the eggs and the sour cream.

I greased and floured the 12-inch Dutch oven and poured in the goo. That went on the coals, as listed above. I turned it every 10–15 minutes.

While it was baking, I rinsed out the 8-inch oven and started on the frosting.

THE FROSTING

TOOLS
8-inch Dutch oven
10–12 coals below

INGREDIENTS
½ cup butter
½ cup milk

¼ cup cocoa
4¼ cups (16-oz. bag) powdered sugar
1 tsp. vanilla extract
¼ cup chunky peanut butter

I STARTED making the frosting by combining the first set of ingredients into the 8-inch Dutch oven and then putting that on some coals. Again, I stirred it occasionally until it boiled. Then I added the rest of the ingredients and stirred it up.

The cake baked for a little over a half hour. When it was done (a toothpick came out clean), I brought it in and let it start to cool in the Dutch oven. After a few minutes, I put a plate on the cake in the Dutch oven and turned it over, tapping it gently on the countertop while holding the plate directly under the cake. It popped out and onto the plate as easy as . . . well . . . a piece of cake.

After it had cooled, I put the frosting on the top. When I sliced and served it, I draped it in a little bit of hot fudge sauce I had. It was a really yummy cake!

DUTCH OVEN BANANA NUT BREAD SUPREME

This was the dessert course at the end of another Mother's Day feast night. It was amazingly delicious. It's a perfect example of how a pretty basic, normal recipe can easily be kicked up a notch and turned into something amazing, without a lot of extra work.

TOOLS
12-inch Dutch oven
8–10 coals below, 15–18 coals above

INGREDIENTS
5 large ripe bananas
4 eggs, well beaten

2 cups sugar
1 cup shortening

4 cups flour
2 tsp. baking soda
1 tsp. baking powder
1 tsp. salt
1 cup chopped nuts (walnuts or almonds or whatever)
2 bars chocolate, chopped

oil
flour

2 sticks butter
1 cup sugar
1–2 Tbsp. cinnamon
chocolate syrup
caramel syrup
whipped cream

I STARTED by puréeing the bananas and added the eggs. Some say that when cooking in a Dutch oven, you should eschew powered appliances. In fact, in many cook-offs, they're not allowed. Usually, I don't use them myself, preferring to do it by hand. But I decided to use the blender on the bananas. May the gods of iron forgive me.

I got over it really fast, though.

Then I got out a bowl and put in the sugar and the shortening. I got out my pastry cutter and started cutting them together. It didn't take long to mix. Then I added the rest of the ingredients from the third set. So far, so good. When choosing the nuts, I picked almonds, because my wife and walnuts don't mix.

And for the chocolate? Ghirardelli! I chose good, good chocolate for an extra special taste.

Finally, I poured in the banana and egg mix and stirred it all together.

I oiled and floured the bottom and sides of my Dutch oven and poured in the mix.

Somewhere, in the process of making everything, I had lit my coals and set a lot of hot coals on the lid to preheat it. When the batter was ready, so was the lid. I put it on and baked the banana bread for 45 minutes to 1 hour, rotating the Dutch oven every 15–20 minutes. I tested its doneness by sticking a toothpick in it. If it comes out clean, then it's done.

Now, I did all this in the morning. There was a lot of other cooking and prepping going on for the rest of the day, so I didn't want to have to rush that. So after I pulled it out of the Dutch oven and cooled it, I wrapped the plate up in plastic so it wouldn't dry out.

Up to this point, it's a good banana bread. But I had to take it to another level. This was to be a fancy dinner, and it needed a fancy ending for that final "Wow!" I decided to dress it up just like I had the Paradise Cookie.

So, right before serving the dessert, I slipped away from dinner. In my 8-inch Dutch oven, I melted the butter, dissolved the sugar, and added the cinnamon. I came back in and sliced up the banana bread into cake-like wedges. I scooped up some of the cinnamon butter sauce, put that in the bottom of a shallow bowl, and added the cake on top of that. Then I drizzled the top of the cake with the chocolate and caramel, making sure to get some drizzled on the bowl too. Finally, a squirrch of whipped cream on top, and it was onto the table.

That little bit of cinnamon and other sauces, combined with the whipped cream, was very simple. But it really took it to another level.

For a few more cool dessert and sweets recipes, go to page 210 and look at the Basic Master Mix recipes.

ADDITIONAL FAMILY RECIPES

CINNAMON APPLE BREAD PUDDING

TOOLS
10-inch Dutch oven inside a 14-inch Dutch oven
11–12 coals below, 22–24 coals above

INGREDIENTS
2 Tbsp. butter
¾ cup brown sugar, divided
1½ tsp. cinnamon, divided
2 apples, cored, peeled, and chopped
2 large eggs
1 (12-oz.) can evaporated milk
¾ cup apple juice
2½ cups bread (french or other), torn into small pieces
1 cup water

MELT THE butter in the 10-inch Dutch oven. Add 2 tablespoons brown sugar, ½ teaspoon cinnamon, and the chopped apples.

In a separate bowl, whisk together the eggs, milk, and apple juice. Add in the remaining sugar and cinnamon and the bread and mix it all.

Add the bread and egg mixture to the butter and spices in the 10-inch Dutch oven.

Pour 1 cup water in the bottom of the 14-inch Dutch oven. Put the 10-inch Dutch oven, without a lid, into the 14-inch. Put the lid on the 14-inch, put it on the coals, and steam/bake it until a test fork comes out clean.

Serve it warm with vanilla ice cream.

BASIC CAKE MIX

When digging through our family recipes, looking for things to add in, I found this series of pages all about making your own basic mixes and storing them for when you want to bake. Great stuff!

INGREDIENTS
10½ cups flour
⅓ cup baking powder
8 cups sugar
½ cup corn starch
1 Tbsp. salt
3 cups shortening

MIX THE dry ingredients, then cut in the shortening with a pastry blending knife. Store it somewhere cool in an airtight container.

Here are the things you can make with the mix: All of these can be baked with the same basic procedure:

TOOLS
10-inch Dutch oven
6–8 coals below, 12–15 coals above

WHISK THE ingredients together. Oil the bottom and sides of the Dutch oven and shake a thin layer of flour over the oil, then pour in the batter.

Put the Dutch oven on the coals to bake. Go for 35–45 minutes, checking it with a toothpick or a fork. Make sure to rotate the Dutch ovens every 15 minutes or so.

When it's done, let it cool, then flip the Dutch oven over, holding a small plate directly under the cake.

Frost it if ya gots it.

YELLOW CAKE

INGREDIENTS
3⅓ cups Basic Cake Mix
2 eggs
¾ cups milk
1 tsp. vanilla

WHITE CAKE

INGREDIENTS
3⅓ cups Basic Cake Mix
3 egg whites
¾ cup milk
1 tsp. vanilla

CHOCOLATE CAKE

INGREDIENTS
9 Tbsp. cocoa
2½ Tbsp. butter
3⅓ cups Basic Cake Mix
2 eggs
1 cup milk

IN THIS case, mix the cocoa and the butter first, then add them to the other ingredients.

Okay, one more from the blog:

ZEBRA CAKE

On my wife's fortieth birthday, I made her a cake. I called it "Zebra Cake," for obvious reasons.

There really isn't a "recipe" per se, since I used boxed cake mixes. It's really just a set of instructions. If you really want to go from scratch (using the basic mixes above), you could do that instead.

TOOLS
2 10-inch Dutch ovens
8–9 coals below each oven, 15–16 coals above each oven

BEGIN BY lighting up the coals and letting them start, then mixing up a bowl of chocolate cake mix according to its directions. After that, mix up a bowl of white cake mix according to its directions.

Give your two Dutch ovens a good blasting of cooking spray or some other good coating of oil and maybe some flour. I just used cooking spray. Using a soup ladle, put in alternating stripes of chocolate batter and white batter until you use all of the batter and divide it pretty evenly between the two Dutch ovens. Then, take a wooden spoon and gently swirl the two batters together in each oven—*not* mixing, but just a little bit of swirling.

Take both Dutch ovens out and set them on the coals. For me, they both cooked only about 35 minutes until I was able to do the toothpick test with each one. When they're done, pull them off the coals and bring them inside.

While they're cooling, take a sheet of foamcore board and cut two circles (a little more than 10 inches in diameter). I put one of the circles directly onto the cake in one of the Dutch ovens and then carefully flipped the oven over while holding onto the foamcore circle. I tapped the oven lightly on the countertop until I could feel the weight of the cake on the circle, then lifted the oven off. the cake was neatly perched on the circle, completely and smoothly removed from the Dutch oven.

I wasn't sure how to handle them at this point, but my wonderful wife clued me in. I wrapped them in aluminum foil and put them in our big freezer.

The next morning, I got them out and opened up a tub of white vanilla frosting and dark chocolate frosting. I laid down some stripes on the top of one cake, then set the other cake right on top of it (without the foamcore, of course). Then I laid some stripes in frosting all over the now-layered cake. When I do this next time, I'll do all the white frosting first. I did the chocolate first this time, and the frosting knife tended to pick up the chocolate and "brown up" the white frosting.

Finally, I broke open bags of white chocolate and milk chocolate chips and meticulously hand-placed the chips on the stripes on the top of the cake.

It was quite a hit at the party. I often got that reaction I'm looking for, you know, that, "You did that in a Dutch oven?" Really, though, it's much simpler than it looks. You mix the mixes, bake the cake, and then stack it and decorate it. When you slice into it, you can see the marbling in the cake itself.

Really, sometimes it's in the cooking, and sometimes it's in the presentation.

CHAPTER 11
HEALTHY DISHES

UNLIKE THE recipes in the last chapters, these are actually good for you!

I know that I said I don't cook in the Dutch oven to be healthy. I know that I don't always make good food choices. Yes, they're often rich and delicious, but they're not always good for me.

A while ago, I read about the concept of "whole foods" cooking. I'm not an expert, but the idea is that if you cook using fresher ingredients, with fewer processes between the farm and your table, your meals will be healthier. Basically, cook stuff that doesn't come from a can or a box. Eat things you have to cut up and stir in.

Now, I can't always meet those criteria, myself. I love pasta, and I love French and Italian white breads. I love chocolate. It's great stuff! But I also can't deny the deliciousness of fresh meats and fresh veggies.

Here's a great one to start things out. There are no special ingredients at all in the list. All whole foods! All low fat, and it looks great!

DUTCH OVEN LIME MARINATED CHICKEN WITH SALSA FRESCA

TOOLS
12-inch Dutch oven
8–9 coals below, 16–17 coals above

INGREDIENTS

The Chicken
4–6 boneless, skinless chicken breasts
juice of 3 limes

2 Tbsp. olive oil
1¼ tsp. ground cumin
liberal shakes of salt and pepper

The Salsa
3 medium tomatoes
1 clove garlic
1 avocado
1 medium onion
3–4 green onions, chopped into the greens
½ cup fresh chopped cilantro
2 jalapenos, seeded and cored
liberal shakes of salt and pepper
leftover marinade from above

IN ONE bowl, I started by mixing all of the ingredients in the first set, except the chicken. I took two teaspoons of the mixture and set it aside in another bowl. I stirred it all up and poured it into a resealable baggie. I added the chicken, shook it all up, and set it aside to marinate in the fridge.

Another idea is to cut the chicken into strips about an inch wide, kinda like stir-fry size.

Once it was thawed and marinated, I put the chicken into a 12-inch Dutch oven. I actually put a fold-out steamer basket in it, because I wanted the chicken juices to drain off, leaving the marinade as a sort of glaze. Since the moisture was still trapped inside the Dutch oven, the chicken didn't dry out.

I put the chicken on the coals. It took only 20 minutes or so to cook. In the meantime, I made the salsa, which was really easy.

I just chopped up all the ingredients, some minced pretty fine, like the cilantro and garlic. I put them into the bowl with the reserved marinade and stirred it all up. I don't remember if I put in more lime juice or not. I would recommend not being stingy with the lime juice.

When the chicken was done, I served it up with the salsa on top and with some seasoned cucumbers. The combination of the hot chicken and the cool salsa, with the lime flavor in both, sure made it taste *great*! My kids just kept ranting on and on about it, and Jodi liked it too. Brendon couldn't believe it was healthy and tasted so good!

WHITE CHILI

Continuing on with my efforts to find and make healthy recipes, I made a white chili. It was interesting to look at. Instead of the dark meat and the deep brown broth, it was very light. A unique twist.

The combination of the leaner meat, the fresh vegetables, and not using anything canned, preprepared, or with preservatives, makes this a healthy alternative.

TOOLS
12-inch Dutch oven
16–20 coals below

INGREDIENTS
1 lb. dry black-eyed peas

1 lb. ground turkey
olive oil
1 large onion
2 cloves garlic

4–6 cups water
2 sweet peppers, one green, one red, diced
1 large tomato, diced
1 jalapeno, diced
4–5 green onions, diced
fresh cilantro, chopped
salt and pepper to taste (In keeping with the white chili theme, I used white pepper.)
juice of 1–2 lemons, to taste (You could even sprinkle the zest when you're serving.)

½ cup corn masa

I ACTUALLY started out, one Tuesday night, by pouring all of the peas (they're beans, really) into a bowl with a lot of water. The water will be absorbed by the beans, so make sure you pour in enough to cover the beans and then double that amount.

The next day, when it was time to cook, I started browning the turkey over 20 or so coals in a 12-inch, shallow Dutch oven. I added a little bit of olive oil at the bottom because I knew that the turkey was much leaner than ground beef and the oil would help the meat to not stick so much.

While the meat was browning, I chopped the onions and minced the garlic. I added a tablespoon or so of olive oil to the Dutch oven and, after a moment, added the onions and garlic to sauté.

Pretty soon, the turkey was done, and the onions were translucent and even a bit browned themselves. I poured the onion/garlic mix into the turkey. Then I

179

added everything in the third set of ingredients except the masa. I drained the beans and added them.

Here's a suggestion in retrospect: Hold back some of the green onions and the fresh cilantro. Maybe as much as half of each. Save them to sprinkle on top of the chili when it's served. That would have looked and tasted great.

The jalapeno I chopped whole, with the veins and seeds. I did it half a pepper at a time. I added some, cooked for a while, tasted, and then added more until I got the heat I wanted. I probably put in only about ¾ of the jalapeno. To me, that was perfect. It was hot but not overpowering. You do it to your taste.

The whole thing cooked about an hour and a half, with 16–20 coals consistently on the bottom. I didn't put any coals on top. I simply added enough to keep it simmering. I only lifted the lid occasionally to stir, check the doneness of the beans, and check the taste with the jalapenos.

The final step was in the last half hour of cooking. I added the corn masa to thicken. This time I didn't add as much as I have in the past. I wanted a thick soup, kind of like a stew, not a paste (which I do like sometimes). I recommend that you do the masa the same way you do the jalapenos. Add some masa and stir it up. Let it cook for a bit, then check to see how thick it is. If it needs more, then add it, and so on.

COOKING A FANCY MEAL FOR MY OWN FATHER'S DAY

WITH STEAMED VEGGIES (THAT'S THE HEALTHY PART)

It was a few years ago that my Dutch oven adventure started. I even have a hard time remembering the scene now. I seem to remember that it was June 2006, Father's Day. We were living in the basement of my in-laws' home at the time, waiting the many months for the completion of the construction on our home. My wife bought me a Lodge 12-inch Dutch oven and gave it to me. I don't remember how I seasoned it, but I got it done and started wondering what I was going to cook in it.

I had pleasant memories of Boy Scout campouts and making pizza. So I decided to try it. It was simple, and it worked, and I was encouraged by my first bits of success. My kids, of course, loved it, because it had pepperoni. I remember I used one of those boxed pizza crust mixes and a jar of Prego for the sauce.

From there, I started cooking pretty much every Sunday, and with few exceptions, that has continued through today. It was nearly eight months later that I began blogging my recipes. I don't see any of that changing in the near future, either. It's been wonderful. I've met a lot of new friends and learned a lot of new skills. It's been a great ride.

So when I cooked up a feast for my own Father's Day, my wife was surprised. It's supposed to be a day off for me. See, she looks at cooking like a chore. I look at it like a break from my crazy week.

I started out thinking I would do that turkey with a southwestern spicy rub that I really liked. I thought, however, that this time I'd brine it first. So the night before, I cleaned out one of our coolers, opened up the turkey, and put it in. Then I covered it up with cool water and mixed in the salt and sugar. Actually, I mixed the salt and sugar in a separate bowl first, to make sure it dissolved right. I left that overnight to soak and to thaw.

I thought I would do another no-knead bread too, so I got the dough ready and set it out to ferment through the day.

The next afternoon, after church, I got things started. After lighting up the coals and getting the turkey on to roast, I got the bread ready. I didn't really do anything fancy. I just followed the recipes as I wrote them!

I did change up the bread in a couple of ways, however. Just after I put the dough into the hot Dutch oven, I sprinkled the top with Parmesan cheese. Lightly, mind you—nothing too oppressive.

Once those were cooking, I was just relaxing and keeping the coals on it. It was a kind of windy day, so I had to keep on top of the coals and keep adding more to the pile in order to keep heat on. But it wasn't a stressful cook at all. The bread took about an hour, and the turkey about three.

The bread, by the way, turned out phenomenal. I finally got a soft crust, with big bubble holes in the crumb! I was so thrilled with myself.

When the turkey was nearly done, I got to thinking about what to serve as a veggie side. I thought about potatoes, and then I suddenly got this idea to do an oven full of steamed mixed veggies. Here's the recipe:

TOOLS
12-inch Dutch oven
15–18 coals below

INGREDIENTS
a bunch of fresh veggies, possibly including:
snow peas
broccoli
red and yellow sweet peppers
cauliflower
2 cups water
light Italian dressing
Parmesan cheese

I CUT up the veggies of various kinds and colors into bite-size bits. I used the ones I listed here, but you could really use anything you've got. Snapped green beans, for example, would be a great addition, as would corn on the cob, snapped into short lengths. I put them in the Dutch oven, on one of those metal, fold-out steamer things, and put in a few cups of water. That went out on the coals.

When they were done, about 45 minutes later, I poured some light Italian dressing over them and sprinkled on some Parmesan cheese. They were delicious and elegant.

At that point, I knew this was more than just a dinner, but a real treat, so I got out our nice dishes, and we all sat down. Turkey, veggies, and bread. What a feast! A great way to celebrate Father's Day, and a special Dutch ovening anniversary!

ADDITIONAL FAMILY RECIPES

CARIBBEAN CHICKEN

This is one that Brendon brought home from school, from his foods class. He cooked it again for us that night and added his own flair. I adapted the instructions for the Dutch oven.

TOOLS
10-inch Dutch oven
16–18 coals below
8-inch Dutch oven
8–10 coals below

INGREDIENTS
1½ tsp. olive oil
4 cups water
2 cups rice
3 boneless chicken breasts or thighs, cut into bite-size pieces
½ cup bottled salsa
1½ tsp. brown sugar
juice from 1 fresh lime
1 (8-oz.) can tomato sauce
a dash of allspice (as much as ¼ tsp.)
salt and pepper to taste
chili powder to taste

GET THE 10-inch Dutch oven on coals, heating up the oil.

Put the 8-inch oven on as well, with the water and the rice in and the lid on. Watch for when the steam starts venting out the sides.

Put the chicken into the 10-inch Dutch oven, and brown.

While the chicken is cooking, mix the remaining ingredients. Add that to the chicken in the 10-inch. Bring it to a boil. Reduce heat by removing 3–4 coals, cover it, and let it simmer at least 5–10 minutes, stirring occasionally.

When the rice starts venting steam, mark that time. About 10 minutes later, pull it off the coals, but don't lift the lid. After 10 or 15 minutes, it's done, and you can lift the lid and fluff it up with a fork.

Serve the chicken over the hot rice.

POTATO BEAN PÂTÉ

Here's another really great one, courtesy of Brendon. He found it in a recipe book one day and made it for us for lunch.

TOOLS
10-inch Dutch oven
15–18 coals below

INGREDIENTS
water sufficient to cover potatoes
2 medium potatoes, diced
2 (15-oz.) cans beans, mixed variety
1 clove garlic, minced or crushed
1 Tbsp. lime or lemon juice
1 Tbsp. chopped fresh cilantro
2 Tbsp. plain yogurt (low fat)
salt
pepper
cilantro
paprika

BOIL THE water in the Dutch oven, then add the potatoes. Boil them until they're tender, then remove them from the water.

Add the potatoes and all the ingredients in the second set to a mixing bowl and mash them together with fork, big spoon, or potato masher.

Serve it spread on crackers or toast, sprinkled with paprika, and with a sprig of cilantro. Very tasty, very fancy, very easy!

CHAPTER 12

BREADS

OVER THE last few years, I've been making a concentrated effort to learn how to make yeast breads in my Dutch ovens. I've tried a lot of variations, like sourdoughs, ryes, sandwich loaves, and even basic french breads. I've checked a lot of recipes, and I've read a lot of books. Few things in Dutch ovening have brought me as much challenge, frustration, and, finally, confidence, as learning how to bake bread.

There's a couple of problems with learning this by study. First of all, a lot of books and recipes assume that you already know the techniques, or at least most of them, so they tell you the ingredients and the proportions, but not how to do it. Second, those books were all about baking bread in a normal oven, or even a specialized baker's oven, not a Dutch oven at a campsite or on your porch (like I do mine).

So through all that study, and trial and error, I've learned some things about bread making. And along the way, I assumed that these were things that everybody knew, and I had just been the slow one. I didn't really talk about it much with people, because I assumed they'd just say, "Well, duh, when did you figure *that* one out?"

But I discovered that many Dutch oven chefs didn't know a lot of the things I was learning, so I started to come out of my shell and share. And I learned even more from the exchange as well.

Now, before I get to a few of my good bread recipes, here are some of the things I've learned. All of these came from my own struggles to get a rich, crusty, soft loaf of bread.

THE RECIPE IS ONLY HALF OF WHAT YOU NEED

Baking good bread is half ingredients and half technique. It's as important to learn how to combine the ingredients and what to do with them as it is to know what ingredients to use. This is where so many simple recipes failed me.

For example, most recipes will tell you to knead and to rise, but none of them told me how to know when I'd kneaded enough or why I sometimes want a slow rise instead of a quick one.

USE FRESH BREAD FLOUR

Bread flour is a higher protein flour, and those proteins combine with water to make gluten, which is the whole basis for yeast breads. The better you do with your gluten, the better it will knead and rise. So trust me. Use bread flour. My family rolls their eyes at me, but it's true, and great bread is the evidence.

It also needs to be fresh. Let me tell you a story, straight from the "pages" of my blog:

Over the last few months, I've tried to make some breads, but they've not worked out well. I first noticed it when I tried to make my sister's whole wheat recipe. It was very difficult to knead it enough to get a good gluten windowpane (see below) going on. After 30–40 minutes, it kinda came together, but not really, and I gave up. It rose, but not as I hoped it would, and when it all baked, it was heavy with a hard crust.

I just figured that it was because that's how whole wheat is, right? But that's not how it was when Mom made it so many years ago . . .

Then my wife tried to make some regular white bread rolls, and they ended up like bricks. I thought to myself, "She didn't knead them enough." Fortunately, I didn't say anything to her, because when I made a white bread a few days later, I had the same problem. And I *was* kneading enough.

I was really down about it. Here I'd been all confident that I was really learning how to make bread, and suddenly nothing was working! I just didn't get it at all!

Gradually it dawned on me that the white flour I'd been using might be bad. It had been a part of my father-in-law's food storage for years, and he had given it to us. I checked with my sister, who's been a wonderful source of inspiration and guidance, and she thought it might be the problem too.

So when I did the bread for the Christmas feast, I bought a fresh bag of bread flour and did it all again, just like I had before. Right away, I could tell a difference. The dough was whiter, where the bad dough had been kind of yellow. It felt better in my fingers as I kneaded it. This was how I remembered it. I got to the point where

I could do a full gluten window in about 10 minutes of kneading.

From then on, I would buy good bread flour in relatively small quantities, so that it wouldn't go months in a bag. I keep it in a dark, sealed container. I protect my bread flour. I've made too many flops, and I don't wanna go there again!

ENRICHMENTS ARE GREAT BUT NOT ALWAYS NECESSARY

Really, all you absolutely need to make bread are four basic ingredients: Flour, salt, yeast, and water. If you can do it with those, you can do it with anything else you wanna add. Sugar, butter, oil, milk, cheese, herbs, nuts, and more all help to make your bread fluffier, tastier, and more unique, but it really all comes down to the basic four. And I've learned that with just those ingredients, you can make a very fluffy and tasty bread!

YOU NEED TO KNEAD

Kneading accomplishes two things on my countertop. One is that I mix in the right amount of flour. Different flours on different days will absorb the water differently. If the dough is dry, it's tough to add more water, but if you make your initial dough wet and sticky and then add more flour as you knead, you can adjust it to the texture you like. I keep adding flour until I can knead it steady without it sticking to my hands. That usually means that I add a little less flour than most recipes call for, and the bread isn't as heavy as a result.

The second reason for kneading is far more important. It develops the gluten strands and makes the bread elastic so that the bread can trap the gas that the yeast makes. That makes the bread rise. For so long, I would be frustrated that my bread wasn't rising. It would take *forever*. I didn't know what was wrong with me. I'd knead the bread as long as the recipe said to, so why wasn't it working?

Just like different flours absorb water differently, they also take varying amounts of kneading. You can't definitively say, "knead for 8 minutes" and know that it'll be enough. You need to do the "windowpane test." That's the only way to know.

THE WINDOWPANE TEST

Cut off a small piece of the dough you're kneading. Roll it into a ball in your palms. Then, working it in a circle, begin to stretch it out flat in the air. Pull it evenly apart, like you're stretching out pizza dough. Keep stretching it thinner and thinner. Watch how long it takes to tear. If you can stretch it out so thin it becomes translucent, like a windowpane, without it tearing, then you've kneaded it enough. If it tears quickly, put that piece back in the dough ball and keep kneading.

PREHEAT THE OVEN

Professional bakers always put their bread into hot ovens. Most Dutch oven bread recipes I read just said to put the bread in your Dutch oven and put some coals on.

Well, sure, eventually, the iron will get hot enough, and it will bake your bread.

However, it turns out that when you shove a ball of dough into an already heated oven, that initial blast of heat will make the dough "spring." That means it puffs up almost immediately. The trapped gas expands, the moisture in the dough turns to steam, and the whole ball just poofs. You get a bigger loaf, with a softer crumb (that's the technical term for the part of the bread that's not the crust).

There are two ways to approach this. One way is to do just what it says: Preheat the Dutch oven. After the bread has risen and you've shaped it, set it aside to proof on a piece or two of baking parchment, with plenty of extra parchment all around the dough. Oil the inside of the Dutch oven. Count out the proper number of coals for baking the bread (according to the recipe). Put the right amount in a ring underneath the Dutch oven, and the right amount above on the lid. Let it sit, empty, while it gets hot and the dough proofs. That could be as much as 20 minutes. Then, when the dough is ready and the Dutch oven is hot, gently lift the dough by the parchment and set it into the Dutch oven. Close the lid and let it bake.

Another method is to preheat the lid of the Dutch oven. After your bread has risen and you've shaped it, put it in an oiled Dutch oven to proof. In the meantime, put some (a lot) of coals on the lid and set it aside. When the loaf is ready, take some of the coals off the lid and put them in a ring on your metal table or on the ground. Set the Dutch oven on the ring of coals, and put the lid on, with the remaining coals. The advantage of this method is that you're not handling the bread as much, so there's less of a chance of degassing the bread as you're trying to maneuver it into a hot Dutch oven. You can also do some fun shapes, like braids and rings. It's much easier to do rolls this way too.

However, the first method gives a better blast of heat and better spring. There are some breads, like french bread, that really only respond to the first method (in my experience).

TURN THE DUTCH OVEN

This is a pretty standard technique that I learned pretty early, and it's vital for bread making. You have to turn the oven from time to time so that you don't get hot spots. Lift the oven and turn it about a quarter turn in one direction, then set it back down on the coals. Then turn the lid about a quarter turn, some say in the opposite direction, but I don't know that it makes any difference. The whole point is to have the placement of the coals different in relation to the bread. This prevents hot spots, which can make the bread cook unevenly.

I usually do it every 15–20 minutes (typically twice during the course of baking a bread loaf), but I know others who do it even more often, every 10–15 minutes. Do it as often as you like, because as long as you don't lift the lid every time and let the heat escape, it won't hurt the bread.

USE A THERMOMETER

It can be difficult to strictly regulate the internal temperature of a Dutch oven. There are sooo many variables. Counting coals is a good idea, but if it's cold out, or windy, or any of a number of factors, the heat can vary. That means that for a long time, I was never sure when it was done. The recipes say to bake for so many minutes, but in a Dutch oven, that's no guarantee. Looking at the "golden brown" of the crust doesn't work, because I can never tell if it's done inside. In a Dutch oven, it's not always practical to reach in, lift out the loaf, and thump it.

My solution? About ⅔ of the way through the baking, I'll lift the lid quickly and stick a meat thermometer in it. Then, some 10 or 15 minutes later, I'll check it. If it's between 180 and 200, it's done. 180 for the lighter types of breads, 200 for heavier breads.

LET IT COOL

Finally, let it cool before cutting it. I used to pull it out and cut it open right away, partly because I was excited, but mostly to be sure it was done. Sadly, it never did seem quite done.

Why? Because much of the final cooking happens as it's cooling! So be patient, let it cool and finish. I used to leave it in the Dutch oven to cool, but I learned that's also counterproductive. It needs to be on cooling racks to develop a nice, soft but dry bottom crust.

So there you have my ideas on making breads in a Dutch oven. Follow the recipe and follow these hints, and at the very least, you'll do better than you did before, I can almost guarantee!

JODI'S SANDWICH LOAF

This bread recipe is one that I've done many times. It's a family favorite. It's a simple, sweet, and soft sandwich loaf (I get bonus blogger points for alliteration). The recipe was given to me by my dear wife, who is also sweet and soft.

TOOLS
12-inch Dutch oven
16–18 coals above, 8–10 below for 350 degrees (in normal weather—more in cold)

INGREDIENTS
1 cup hot water
¾ cup honey
1 Tbsp. yeast
4–5 cups flour, with probably about a cup or two to be added during kneading
a pinch of salt
1 cup milk (mixed from powder)
1 egg
2 Tbsp. oil

spray oil
an egg to coat the top

FIRST, I activate the yeast. I get fully hot tap water and add the honey to it. This cools it significantly, but it's still quite warm. I add the yeast to that and let it sit and grow foamy for a while.

Then, in a separate bowl, I add the flour and the other ingredients. I add in the yeast/honey mix and stir it all up with a wooden spoon. The dough will come loose from the sides of the bowl but still be quite sticky.

Then I flour up the countertop and dump the dough out. I sprinkle more flour onto the dough ball and start kneading. It's still quite sticky, but I keep kneading and sprinkling on more flour gradually until it no longer consistently sticks to my fingers and the table.

Then I keep kneading until I can make a good windowpane, like it says above. Once it's ready, I use spray oil on the mixing bowl and put the dough back in. I spray another coating of oil on top to keep it from drying out, cover it with a towel, and set it aside to rise.

Once it has risen, I go outside and start up the coals. It will take a while for the coals and the oven to get ready for me to proof the bread.

I come back in and dump out the dough. Using one of those cool pastry cutters, I cut it into quarters and form each quarter into a ball. I pull the surface around and underneath, then pinch it together at the bottom. That stretches the surface smooth. I quickly spray oil into the Dutch oven and put each dough ball on the bottom, as if the Dutch oven had been divided in quarters. Then I set the Dutch oven aside to rise again (proofing).

In the meantime, I take the Dutch oven lid outside and pour some coals onto it, about 20 or so, so it will preheat. After about 20 minutes, the dough balls have risen some, and I know the lid is good and hot. I coat the top of the dough balls with the beaten egg. Then, outside, I make a ring of coals, set the Dutch oven onto it, and close the lid.

I let it cook for about an hour. Every 15 minutes or so, I rotate the lid about a quarter turn and then lift and turn the oven itself. This helps reposition the coals relative to the oven and the bread inside so you don't get hot spots. After about a half hour, I put a cooking thermometer into the dough and reclose the lid. That allows me to check the internal temperature of the bread. Soft breads like this are done at 180–200 degrees Fahrenheit.

When it's done, I pull it off and, using hot pads, shake the bread out of the ovens. I let it cool on cooling racks.

IRISH SODA BREAD

As I mentioned before, I've been working on and learning how to do breads for several years. I've done sourdoughs, whites, ryes, sweets, whole wheats, herbals, and so on. I've done all kinds of breads.

But the one kind of bread that always challenged me was the traditional Irish soda bread. For the longest time, it always failed. Most of my attempts would turn out like bricks. Sometimes the inner crumb would be fairly soft, but even that was usually pretty dense, and the crust would be like a suit of armor.

I studied and researched and tried very hard to figure out why it wasn't working. I saw many recipes, and many of the ones that looked light and fluffy read more like cake recipes than bread, with lots of sugar and eggs. It just didn't seem like the Irish soda bread I was shooting for. Crusty is fine, as long as it's still soft to the teeth. I wanted it to puff up and brown in the oven. I also was shooting for a crumb that had air bubbles in it—not huge ones, but enough to make it easy to eat.

I remember that I came across one website where someone clearly had an ax to grind, as he was trying to preserve the concept of a "traditional Irish soda bread" (sodabread.info). The site owner was quite clear on what was a proper Irish soda bread, and what was not.

The problem is that, even with all this study and learning, my soda loaves still would turn out as if they could easily be used to grind axes. While that may be practical, that didn't make them any more palatable, even with butter and jam.

I did learn, however, that Dutch ovens (or something like them) were often used to bake traditional soda bread. They were big, cast iron pots that often had sharp bumps on the underside of the lid. When cooking, especially when cooking meats, the steam would gather on these points and drip back down onto the meat. This earned them the name "bastibles."

I just didn't feel like I could claim any authority as a Dutch oven bread baker if I couldn't do a decent chemically leavened bread. I knew that it *could* be done in a Dutch oven, but I just couldn't seem to pull it off.

Until one day, all of that research and study came together, and it *worked*!

TOOLS
12-inch Dutch oven
10–12 coals below, 20–24 coals above

INGREDIENTS
2 full cups flour
1 tsp. salt
1 slightly heaped tsp. cream of tartar
1 heaped tsp. baking soda
1 cup (full ½-pint carton) buttermilk

I STARTED by lighting the coals. Once those were showing some good white burn, I set the Dutch oven (with a spritz of oil on the inside) on and under the coals. This will be a lot of heat. While that was preheating, I set about making the dough. It goes really quickly.

I added all of the dry ingredients together in a bowl. After measuring the flour, I sifted it, mainly to aerate it. Notice, also, that I didn't use bread flour. In my studies, I've learned that chemical leavens don't rely on gluten strands to trap the gas and rise, like yeast breads do. Instead, the chemicals interact and create the gas, which is trapped by the liquid and the fats in the buttermilk. It's also the acids in the buttermilk reacting with the soda that produces the gas in the first place.

Back to the process . . .

Then I made a well in the middle of all the powders, poured in the buttermilk, and gradually stirred it in. Soon, it was clumping together. I reached in with my fingers, kneaded it in the bowl, and shaped it. This is a very important part: don't work it too much. It's *not* a yeast bread, where you're kneading it for 20 minutes or more. A few squeezes and folds to mix it well and a bit of shaping and molding, and you're ready to go. The more it interacts with your hands, the warmer it gets, and you want it cold.

I shaped the dough into a flat disk about 6 inches around by about 1½ inches high. This is another important part. I don't know how I missed this, but in the past, I always shaped it into a high and rounded ball. I think that had a big, big impact on how much it rose up and how the heat could cook into the bread. Pressing it into a flat disk gives it less bulk and makes it better able to rise up in the baking.

There are all kinds of stories about why this bread is traditionally cut with a cross on top. I'm a kind of practical guy, so I know why I did it. One, it allows the bread to spring up and spread. Two, it gives it a place to vent a lot of the steam as it bakes. And three, it makes it very easy to break into four even pieces once it's done.

Finally, I put it into the Dutch oven. It looked kinda small and pathetic when I put it in, actually. It made me think that next time, I'd probably double the recipe or cook it in the 10-inch oven instead.

I ended up cooking it about 40 minutes, I think. I would recommend it be cooked to an internal temperature of 160–180 degrees. The first one I did, I cooked to 190, and it was a little too crusty, I think, especially on the bottom. Resist the urge to add too many coals underneath, by the way. Watch the bottom coals, and do some replenishing so they don't burn out, but don't go crazy with it.

193

Overall, I've learned that traditional Irish soda bread is a totally different animal from yeast breads. In order for me to successfully make it, I had to separate myself from much of what I had learned about yeast bread making. They are different processes and should not be confused.

COOK–OFF BUTTER ROLLS

I can easily remember my first cook-off. I was pretty green to the whole world of Dutch oven cooking and had never cooked publicly or in competition before. The cook-off was at a pretty simple hometown fair. We had to prepare two dishes: a main dish and a bread. The main dish I did was the baked salmon and rice found in the seafood section of this book, on page 85.

This was the bread I chose. Even though, at the time, I didn't really know much about making breads, it still came out pretty well. I can remember the crumb being a bit more dense than I'd wanted, but the crust (particularly the upper) was perfectly browned and soft.

TOOLS
12-inch Dutch oven
7 coals below, 14 coals above

INGREDIENTS
1 Tbsp. yeast
½ cup warm water
1 cup melted butter (melt a half cup first, then another half later on)
½ cup sugar
2 eggs
1 tsp. salt
1 cup milk
5+ cups flour

I STARTED by mixing the yeast and the water, and I let it stand for 15 minutes or so, to activate the yeast and foam up.

In my mixing bowl, I added ½ cup of the melted butter, the eggs, the sugar, and the salt. Then I added the milk and stirred it all up. Finally, I added the yeast and water. All of the wet mix was done.

Next, I added 5 cups of flour, stirring as I went to make a smooth dough ball. I added more as needed to get the right consistency. The original recipe didn't say to, but that day, I remember I kneaded it in the bowl for 5 minutes or so. This is one of the problems I have with so many bread recipes. They don't teach you about how long to knead or how to tell, like I did above.

I covered the dough with a damp cloth and set the mixing bowl somewhere warm (in the summer, I just use the back porch) for a couple of hours. The day of the cook-off was pretty warm, but when I was mixing the dough, it still had some morning chill. I set it in the sun. I let the dough ball double in bulk.

When it had risen, I broke off chunks somewhere between the size of a golf ball and a tennis ball, rolled them, and arranged them in the bottom of my buttered Dutch oven. Then I spread the other ½ cup of melted butter liberally over the dough balls. I put that out on the coals and baked it for about 45 minutes to an hour. At the time, I hadn't learned about preheating the oven. They still turned out great but, as I said, a bit dense.

A tricky part about baking, I've discovered, is heat management. It's got to be hot, but if it's too hot, then the bread burns on the top and bottom and is still doughy in the middle. If it's not hot enough, it never cooks at all. The sad thing is, I don't think you can learn how to regulate it by reading a book. The only way is to try it on your own, following the directions and counting as close as you can, and see how it works. It took me many tries to make really good bread. Fortunately, this recipe was one of the winners!

Also, any time I'm cooking more than 45 minutes or so, I've found that I have to add more coals. I keep a stack of burning briquettes off to the side of my cooking area and replenish it by 4–5 coals at a time, just to keep a good fresh supply and maintain the heat on the ovens.

It is *critical* to turn the oven every 15 minutes or so. Just lift the oven by the wire and turn it about a quarter turn, then turn the lid a quarter turn back the other direction. This assures that the bread isn't over or under the same hot spots for the whole baking period. Another thing I did was cook the last 15 or so minutes with top heat only.

BISCUITS

When I make soup, I always get this urge to make biscuits along with it. Especially those thick, hot comfort soups like split pea or chowder (pages 102 and 231, respectively). It just makes it more of a complete meal.

Much of what I learned earlier about making the soda bread applies to making biscuits too, since they're both a chemical leaven. Don't work it too much, keep it cool, don't make it too tall, and so on. All are good to keep in mind.

Here are a few fun biscuit recipes.

A BASIC BISCUIT RECIPE

TOOLS
12-inch, shallow Dutch oven
12 coals below, 20 coals above

INGREDIENTS
2 cups flour
1 Tbsp. baking powder (double-acting)
½ tsp. salt
½ cup shortening
¾ cup milk

NO MATTER what kind of biscuits I'm making, I usually follow a similar process. I start by lighting up the coals. I let them get a bit white while I gather up the ingredients and prepare my space.

Then, when the coals are white, I put the Dutch oven (with some oil spritz) on and under the burning coals to preheat while I mix and prepare the dough. If I'm making a big batch, I might even heat up two Dutch ovens.

I start off by mixing all of the dry ingredients. After measuring the flour, I sift it, primarily to aerate it. Then I add the shortening and cut it in using a pastry cutter. Once that's well blended, I add in the milk and mix it up with a big spoon. I even reach my hand in a few times and mix that way, with kind of a kneading motion, but I don't do that too much. With biscuits, as with soda bread, you don't want to develop any gluten, and you don't want the fats to get warm and soft. They need to trap the gas the chemical reaction is making.

Then I dump it out on the floured counter and flatten it out (either with a rolling pin, if I can find one, or my hands). I flatten it to ½–¾ of an inch. I sprinkle on some flour and fold it over. Then I flatten it out again. I repeat this process 4–5 times, creating layers. Still, don't do this too much. The first chemical reaction has already been taking place, and you don't want to wait around too much.

I cut them into circles. I'm told that if you use a cup, you shouldn't twist it, because it can let too much gas out. I've never noticed it that much. After punching out a few circles, wad the remaining dough back up, flatten it again, and cut some more.

At various times, I've coated the tops with milk, butter, or beaten egg. They will give different textures and browning.

Then I take the biscuit rounds out and put them in the ovens. I check them after about 10 minutes, at which point, if they're not done, they should be pretty close. Then enjoy them with butter and jam or honey!

DUTCH OVEN WHIPPING CREAM BISCUITS

TOOLS
12-inch, shallow Dutch oven
12 coals below, 20 coals above

INGREDIENTS
4 cups flour
2 Tbsp. baking powder (not heaping, but not level either)
4 tsp. sugar
3 tsp. salt
3 (½-pint) cartons heavy whipping cream

THE PROCESS is the same as above, even though the quantities are much higher. Notice that you're not adding any shortening or butter, but the heavy whipping cream has plenty of fat.

SODA POP BISCUITS

TOOLS
12-inch Dutch oven
12 coals below, 20 coals above

INGREDIENTS
3 cups flour
⅜ cup oil
1 (12-oz.) can lemon-lime soda pop (I used 7-Up, and not the diet stuff, either.)
3 Tbsp. baking powder

FOLLOW THE procedure above. If it ends up being a little sticky, sprinkle in a little more flour. This dough is so light and airy that I don't have to roll it out. I just spread it out with my hands on the floured tabletop. I spread it to about ¾-inch thick and cut it with a drinking cup.

Take them outside, put them in the heated oven, and start the baking. After half an hour to 40 minutes, take the oven off the bottom coals but leave the coals on the lid so the tops will brown without burning the bottoms.

PIZZA

One of the earliest comments on my blog was on one of my earliest postings. I had mentioned that I'd done really good pizza, and she asked, "So cool . . . how did you do it? Our goal in Dutch oven cooking is the perfect pizza."

The secret is actually pretty easy, and not really much of a secret. The answer demonstrates an important principle I've been learning about cooking, especially with the Dutch oven. That principle is GIGO.

Those of you who are into computers, especially in programming, already understand this term. For the rest of us in the real world, it means "Garbage In, Garbage Out." In the culinary world, it means that if you make a dish with garbage, it's going to taste like garbage. The opposite is also true, and that's really the main point. If you use good stuff to make your food, it will taste great. So, to make good pizza, don't scrimp on your ingredients. A good dough recipe, good sauce, and good toppings make great pizza. Really, that's pretty much common sense, but sometimes we forget.

The first time I made pizza, I just used a pizza crust mix and bottled spaghetti sauce. It turned out pretty well, but not amazing. From then on, I've always made my own and used the best and freshest toppings I could find. That makes all the difference.

I can remember one particular Friday, as I was coming home from work, I was kinda hankering to cook something on the back porch in the Dutch ovens. As I drove home, I was a little bit deterred by the drops of rain on my windshield and the "wikk, wikk, wikk" of my wipers. But I decided to go for it anyway.

I didn't want to do anything complex or fancy this time, so I decided on pizza. It had been a really long time since I'd last done that. My wife's not a big fan of pizza, so whenever I suggest it, she comes up with other ideas. But she was working late that night.

On the way, I stopped at the store and bought some supplies. Pepperoni, Canadian bacon, mozzarella, olives . . . We already had onions and peppers. I'm a supreme combo pizza kinda guy.

TOOLS
2 12-inch Dutch ovens
8–10 coals below, 16–18 coals above
(In this case, because of the rain, I did the coals differently, as you'll read.)

INGREDIENTS

The Crust
1½ cups warm water
1 Tbsp. yeast

1 Tbsp. sugar
¼ tsp. salt
3 Tbsp. olive oil
about 4 cups flour
cooking spray

I STARTED by putting the yeast in some of the warm water to let it foam up. My experience has shown me that things tend to rise very slowly or poorly in my house (could be the altitude), so I sprinkle a little extra yeast.

I mixed the other ingredients in a bowl, added the water and the yeast, and kneaded it into a ball (remember to use the windowpane test, written at the start of this chapter). I also put in a little extra sugar to help the extra yeast along. I used the last bit of flour to adjust the smoothness of the dough. Not too dry, not too sticky. You might not use exactly 4 cups. I sprayed the bowl with cooking spray, put the dough ball in it, and then sprayed the top of the dough. I set that aside to raise.

After about a half hour to 45 minutes of twiddling my thumbs and watching lame TV on the Disney Channel (my kids were home), I went outside and lit up about 50 coals or so. At that moment, it wasn't raining, so I was doing okay. Once the coals were glowing, I scattered them into two groups and put two 12-inch Dutch ovens on. I split a pound of mild Italian sausage between the two ovens and let that start to brown. Pretty soon it was drizzling, so I put lids on the ovens.

In the meantime, I mixed up the sauce.

The Sauce
1 (8-oz.) can tomato sauce
1 (6-oz.) can tomato paste
1 Tbsp. dried onions
1 Tbsp. black pepper
1 Tbsp. celery salt
1 Tbsp. oregano (maybe a little more)
1 Tbsp. basil

Actually, those amounts on the spices are estimates. Just go until it smells rich!

MY TIMING was good. Just about the time that the sausage was browned, the dough had risen enough. I brought the Dutch ovens inside and pulled the sausage out. In the bottom of each oven, now well-greased from the sausage, I added some minced garlic (about a tablespoon), a bit of butter (about a tablespoon), and some shakings of celery salt. The butter melted nicely, and I spread the seasonings around the bottom of the pan. This gives a crispy and flavorful bottom to the crust.

I took the now-risen ball of dough, split it in half, and formed one half into the pizza flat. That went into the bottom of one Dutch oven. The other half of the dough did the other Dutch oven.

Onto that went the sauce and a thin layer of cheese. I had bought one of those shredded Italian cheese blends, with mozzarella, provolone, Parmesan, and Romano. Mmmmmm . . .

Then I piled on the toppings—the sausage, Canadian bacon, pepperoni, fresh sliced onions, olives, and so on! In my book, the more, the merrier. And finally, I layered the whole thing with a pretty thick blanket of cheese. I was doing this all as fast as I could, since the coals were outside getting rained on.

So I took the ovens back outside. I have this big, round metal hood that's designed to shelter Dutch ovens, so I decided to use it. I put about 12 coals in a circle and put an oven on top of that. Then I put about 14 coals on top of that oven. I stacked the second oven on top and put roughly 14 coals on that one. Then the whole thing went under the hood.

After about 15 minutes, I unstacked them, turned them, and restacked them to distribute the heat more evenly. It was raining pretty steadily but not heavily the whole time. Finally, after about 35 minutes, it was done! And it was snowing!

Dang yummy pizza, and very filling!

PHILLY STEAK SANDWICHES

One spring, while I was at a family party, one of my sisters-in-law made some steak sandwiches. She bought the buns and made the meat and sauce in her slow cooker. It was delicious! Well, my mind instantly went to the Dutch oven. I started thinking of how I could make the same thing. But just doing the meat and the veggies would be too easy, of course. I needed to challenge myself. So I decided that I would make the buns too.

THE ROLLS

TOOLS
2 12-inch, shallow Dutch ovens
10 coals below, 20 coals above

INGREDIENTS
5 tsp. yeast (2 packets)
3 cups water (½ cup to start, 2½ cups later)
2 Tbsp. sugar (1 to start, 1 later)
¼ cup vegetable oil
1 Tbsp. salt
about 8 cups flour (4 at first, and add the rest as you knead)

I STARTED by mixing a half cup of warm water with the yeast and a tablespoon of sugar. I left it to foam up, and it did pretty readily (about 5 minutes).

Then, in a mixing bowl, I put the rest of the water, the rest of the sugar, the oil, and the salt. To that, I added the yeast mixture.

I dumped in the first 4 cups of flour and started mixing. It was quite sticky, of course, as I stirred. I started adding the rest of the flour a cup at a time, stirring and mixing as I went. I used pretty much the full 8 cups. After it had stirred, I started kneading it until it all stuck together in a ball. Then I pulled it out of the bowl, set it onto the floured table, and started kneading in earnest. I kneaded for 5–6 minutes (always checking for a good windowpane), sprinkling on a little bit of flour as needed to keep it from sticking. I scraped out the bowl, sprayed it with oil, and put in the dough ball. I finished that off by spraying the top of the dough and covering it all with a plastic bag.

After about 45 minutes, I was surprised to see how much it had risen. So I started the coals on fire. Then I dumped out the dough and punched it down. I cut it into 10 or 12 equal pieces, then I rolled them in my hands into a torpedo shape and cut diagonal slices across the top to allow the steam to escape the bread. I put them into the two 12-inch Dutch ovens as best I could. I tried to make at least an empty inch between each long dough ball. While these were proofing and rising in the Dutch ovens, I got hot coals on the lids to preheat them.

202

Finally, I put them on the coals. It took a good 30 coals for each oven. I also had a few left over, and I added more to that so I'd have enough hot coals for . . .

THE MEAT

TOOLS
10-inch Dutch oven
15–18 coals below

INGREDIENTS
1–1½ lbs. finely sliced steak beef. I used "stir-fry" beef, but I'm told you can get any cut of beef sliced Philly-style.
1–2 Tbsp. oil
liberal shakes of steak seasoning mix
2 medium onions
1 green bell pepper
1 red bell pepper
1 jalapeno
2–3 Tbsp. freshly chopped chives
1 cup fresh sliced mushrooms
liberal shakes of salt
a little water
1–2 Tbsp. flour

I PUT the 10-inch Dutch oven on a bed of coals and packed them in underneath as best I could. Then I dumped in the meat pieces with the oil. I just cooked that, browning it, with a bit of stirring until it was pretty much cooked through. I also added the steak seasoning here.

While that was cooking, in between stirrings, I jumped inside and sliced up the veggie ingredients. The jalapenos I sliced pretty thin and halved. I don't like to get a big bite of chili surprise, but I do like the edge it gives the rest of the food. I put all the veggies in, stirred it all up, and salted it to taste. I cooked it, covered, and stirred it occasionally.

Meanwhile, the bread was cooking. The coal count should have brought it up to 400 degrees. I baked it for about a half hour. After that, I pulled the Dutch ovens off the bottom coals and let the rolls continue baking with just the top heat. When they were done, I let them sit in the hot ovens, after I took the top heat off, for about another 5 minutes or so, just to let them finish. Then I took them out of the pots to let them cool and air out a little bit.

By this time, the veggies were cooked down pretty nicely. There was some water in it from the veggies and the meat, so I sprinkled on a little flour to thicken it up. My wife suggested a bit more "sauce" as we were eating, so I included the suggestion of a little water in the Dutch oven as it's cooking. But I'm not convinced it needed it.

Finally, it was all ready to serve! We sliced open the buns, added a little mayo and mustard (not too much or it competes with the meat's own flavor), and topped it with some swiss cheese. I was amazed. I think it was one of the best hot sandwiches I have ever tasted.

MONKEY BREAD

Many people make monkey bread by taking canned "pop-up" biscuits, rolling them in cinnamon sugar, and then baking them. Then you stack them randomly in your Dutch oven and bake them. That's easy enough, but I love making things from scratch. I also love yeast bread, so this recipe takes that approach.

I made these for an Easter celebration at a friend's house one year. I figured that the small rolls, tightly bunched together, would allow many people to just grab a bit of them and enjoy!

TOOLS
12-inch Dutch oven
10–12 coals below, 20–24 coals above

INGREDIENTS
2 Tbsp. yeast
2 cup water (at about 110 degrees)
¾ cup sugar
5–6 cups flour
1½ tsp. salt
1 cup butter
2 eggs

some sugar
2 Tbsp. ground cinnamon
oil

FIRST, I activated the yeast by stirring it into the water in a cup. While that was getting all bubbly, I mixed, in a bowl, all of the dry ingredients except the sugar and cinnamon, but only about 4 cups of the flour to start. After measuring the flour, I sifted it. I've gotten into the habit of doing that. It aerates the flour, and I think it's a bit lighter as a result.

Then I got out my pastry cutter and cut in the butter. I guess another option would be to melt the butter into the powders. Either way.

Finally, I added the eggs and the yeast mixture. I stirred it all together, then turned it out onto a floured countertop and kneaded until I got a good window-pane (see p. 187). Once it was all kneaded, I set it aside to rise.

In about 2 hours, it was nicely risen. I mixed some sugar into the cinnamon until it looked like a nice blend and it tasted right. I started pinching off dough balls about the size of ping-pong balls, rolled them in the cinnamon sugar, and put them into the oiled Dutch oven. I didn't worry much about the placement; I just scattered them evenly. After putting them in, I sprinkled the rest of the cinnamon sugar over the top.

Once the dough balls were done, I started up some coals, and when those were getting white, I put a lot of them (25–30) on the lid of the Dutch oven to preheat it. That was heating while the dough was rising a second time in the body of the Dutch oven. Once they both were ready, I put the Dutch oven out on (and under) the right amount of coals and baked them for about an hour. I used the thermometer and got them to the 190–200 range.

I didn't pay as much attention to the upper heat, and it got a little burned on top. I think the extra sugar on top had a lot to do with that as well. Still, they were sure yummy, and everyone at the party loved them.

PARMESAN SEASONED BREADSTICKS

One time, when I was making pasta, my wife suggested I make some breadsticks with seasonings and parmesan cheese. She showed me this recipe in an old church cookbook. I admit I was a bit skeptical. It was a yeast bread recipe, but the rise time was really short and the instructions were really strange. But I decided to give it a shot. I was glad I did.

TOOLS
12-inch Dutch oven
12 coals below, 22 coals above

INGREDIENTS
1½ cups warm water
1 Tbsp. yeast
1 Tbsp. honey
1 tsp. salt
about 4 cups flour
¼ cup butter, melted
liberal shakes of Parmesan cheese and other seasonings

FIRST, IN a bowl, I put the water, yeast, and honey together and let the yeast activate. Then I added the salt and the flour. Don't add all the flour at once, because then you can gauge the moistness and the density of the dough. I kneaded it for 10 minutes.

Then I poured the melted butter in the bottom of the 12-inch oven and spread the dough out over it. I cut the dough into strips, then sprinkled the parmesan and the seasonings (I used this really great salad seasoning combo) on top. This is where I was really skeptical. At that point, I set it aside for about 20 to 30 minutes to rise. That's it. No long rise or proofing.

Finally, once it had risen some, I put it on the coals. In about 20 minutes to a half hour, they were done. And they were delicious! Who knew?

And the penne came out incredible too. It was really filling, and wow, what a dinner!

CONFERENCE CINNAMON ROLLS

Twice a year, in April and October, my church's main headquarters in Salt Lake City hosts a two-day conference. There are five sessions, and four of them are televised. Outside of the Utah area, not all of the sessions are broadcast. When I was growing up in Indiana, our local station carried only the Sunday morning session. So those Sundays became very special to me. We got to go to church at home and watch church in our jammies!

We also had a tradition of baking something delicious in the morning as we listened. It would vary from year to year, but one in particular that I remember was cinnamon rolls. So one conference Sunday, I decided to revive that old tradition.

TOOLS
12-inch Dutch oven
8–9 coals below, 16–17 above

INGREDIENTS
1 Tbsp. dry yeast
½ cup warm water
½ cup warm milk
⅓ cup sugar
⅓ cup shortening
1 tsp. salt
1 egg

3–4 cups flour

2 Tbsp. softened butter
¼ cup sugar
2 tsp. ground cinnamon
a small handful of brown sugar
a few shakes of ground ginger

I GOT up really early and started this off. I let the yeast activate and foam up in the water. I added all the other ingredients in the first block and mixed all that up. Then I started adding in the flour, a cup or two at a time. I don't remember exactly how many it took for me this time.

Then I started kneading it on the table. I added shakes of flour onto the table as I went along. I've learned that in the past I've not been kneading it enough. This time, as with the last time I made a yeast bread, I kneaded it until I felt it loosen up. It takes a while, maybe 8–10 minutes.

Then I set it aside to rise.

It rose slowly and took about an hour and a half to double. Once it had doubled, I put it back on the floured tabletop and rolled it out flat, into a square (or as close to it as I could get). I spread the butter over the surface and sprinkled it with the mix of cinnamon and sugar.

Then I rolled it up and sliced it into 1-inch lengths. I set these into an oiled 12-inch, shallow Dutch oven. Once all those rolls were in the oven, I set it aside to rise. That took about another 40 minutes.

Even with that, it didn't really rise like I'd expected it to. I sprinkled the brown sugar over the tops of the risen rolls and then shook some ground ginger on top of that. Not much, though.

I put that on the coals and let it bake for about 40 minutes. When it was all done, they were delicious!

ADDITIONAL FAMILY RECIPES

BASIC MASTER MIX FOR QUICK BREADS AND CAKES

When I was young, one time my mom was showing me some cooking skills. She mixed up this batch of stuff and put it in a large plastic jar she had. I can clearly remember her smiling at me while she wrote with a permanent marker in big letters "BASIC MIX" on the side of the jar. She explained that it could be used to make a lot of different things. Pretty much anything short of world peace. Then we used a bit of it to make pancakes.

Being the smart aleck I was, from that moment on, our family referred to pancakes as "basics," because they'd been made from "basic mix."

Then I found a variation on the same idea in the stack of recipes that my wife had kept in her family. I add them here, slightly adapted for Dutch oven use.

First you have to make the Basic Master Mix, from which all the other goodness will spring. Then you store it and use it as the basis for so many other baking and quick bread recipes.

INGREDIENTS
5 lbs. flour (20 cups)
2½ cups powdered milk
¾ cup double-acting baking powder
3 Tbsp. salt
2 Tbsp. cream of tartar
½ cup sugar
1 lb. vegetable shortening

SIFT OR whisk all the ingredients (except the shortening) together. Mix well, because the entire quantity needs to be an even balance of all ingredients.

Use a pastry cutter to cut in the shortening until it looks well blended, like cornmeal.

Store it in large resealable bags or another airtight container in a cool, dry place. It keeps well for 6–8 weeks.

USING THE BASIC MASTER MIX

PANCAKES

TOOLS
12-inch Dutch oven lid
18–22 coals below

INGREDIENTS
3 cups Basic Master Mix (BMM)
1 egg
1½ cups water (adjust to the consistency you like)
oil

MIX INGREDIENTS all except the oil) well with a whisk. Preheat a Dutch oven lid on a lid stand over 18–22 coals. Spritz it with oil. Pour on the batter, and cook for a few minutes on each side. For more on pancakes, see pages 147 and 156.

BISCUITS

TOOLS
12-inch Dutch oven
12–15 coals below, 24–28 coals above

INGREDIENTS
oil
3 cups BMM
¾ cup water

PREHEAT THE Dutch oven, spritzed with oil. Blend the BMM and the water. Mix it and roll it out on a table. Cut it into circles and place them in the Dutch oven. Bake them for 10–15 minutes.

MUFFINS

I'm not sure how you would get a muffin tin in a Dutch oven, but I'll include the recipe here, anyway.

INGREDIENTS
3 cups BMM
2 Tbsp. sugar
1 egg
1 cup water

MIX ALL the ingredients. Bake it at 450 degrees for 25 minutes. Pretty simple, really!

GINGERBREAD BARS

TOOLS
12-inch Dutch oven
8–10 coals below, 16–20 coals above

INGREDIENTS

2 cups BMM
¼ cup sugar
½ tsp. cinnamon
½ tsp. ground ginger
½ tsp. ground cloves
1 egg
½ cup water
½ cup molasses

PREHEAT THE Dutch oven lid with lots of coals. Mix the dry ingredients, then add the wet ingredients. Roll it out thin, and press and shape into the base of the Dutch oven. Put the Dutch oven on and under coals. Bake for 45–50 minutes and then cut into squares or wedges.

BASIC CAKE

TOOLS

12-inch Dutch oven
8–10 coals below, 16–20 coals above
You could use a 10-inch Dutch oven. The cake will come out thicker, and you'd use slightly fewer coals (maybe 7–9 below and 14–18 above).

INGREDIENTS

3 cups BMM
1¼ cups sugar
2 eggs
1 tsp. vanilla
1 cup water
oil
flour

PREHEAT THE Dutch oven lid with lots of coals.

Mix the Basic Master Mix and sugar well.

Add the eggs, vanilla, and water and whisk vigorously or blend for 2–3 minutes. Oil and flour the Dutch oven and pour in the batter.

Put it on and under the coals and bake for 20–30 minutes, or until a toothpick inserted comes out clean.

When it's cooled, place a plastic plate, inverted, over the cake in the Dutch oven. Holding the plate in place, invert the Dutch oven. Shake or tap the oven to dislodge the cake onto the plate. Frost it or serve as desired.

COFFEE CAKE

TOOLS
12-inch Dutch oven
12–15 coals below, 24–28 coals above
As above, you could use a 10-inch Dutch oven. The cake will come out thicker, and
   you'd use slightly fewer coals (maybe 7–9 below and 14–18 above).

INGREDIENTS
3 cups BMM
1/2 cup sugar

1 egg
2/3 cup water

oil
flour

1/2 cup brown sugar
3 Tbsp. butter
1/2 tsp. cinnamon

nuts
raisins
chocolate chips

PREHEAT THE Dutch oven lid with lots of coals. Mix the first set of dry ingredients, then add the second set of wet ingredients. Blend well. Oil and flour
the Dutch oven and pour in the batter. Mix the next set of ingredients (the last
set of ingredients is optional), and sprinkle it on top of the batter. Bake it for 25
minutes.

Let it cool. When cooled, flip the cake onto a plate using the technique in the
previous recipe.

COOKIE BARS

TOOLS
12-inch Dutch oven
8–10 coals below, 16–20 coals above

INGREDIENTS
3 cups BMM
1 cup sugar
1 egg
1 tsp. vanilla
1/3 cup water

Enhancements
chocolate chips
nuts
raisins
oatmeal

PREHEAT THE Dutch oven lid with lots of coals. Mix the dry ingredients, add in the wet ingredients, and blend them well. Add in any enhancements you like. Spread it all out on the bottom of the Dutch oven. Put it on and under coals and bake it for 10–15 minutes. Cut it into bars or wedges for serving.

DUMPLINGS

TOOLS
Any Dutch oven, already simmering with soup or stew

INGREDIENTS
2 cups BMM
½ cup water

MIX THE ingredients and drop by spoonfuls onto the simmering stew toward the end of the cooking time. Cover the Dutch oven and cook for an additional 15–20 minutes. Serve.

SEAFOOD FONDUE

Okay, I know this is *technically* not a bread. But I love to make this and bake up one of my loaves of bread. Then we tear apart the bread, and everybody dips into the fondue. It's great fun and a great taste!

TOOLS
10-inch Dutch oven
16–18 coals below

INGREDIENTS
½ cube butter
flour
2 cups milk
½ tsp. cayenne
½ tsp. paprika
1 red bell pepper, chopped
1–2 cans crab/shrimp/other seafood, drained
8 oz. grated cheese
2 Tbsp. fresh parsley

START BY getting the Dutch oven on coals and melting the butter. Add the flour, 1–2 tablespoons at a time, until it looks like loose cookie dough. Cook it, stirring, for 10–15 minutes. You now have a blond roux. Remove it from the Dutch oven.

Add the milk, the seasonings, the bell pepper, and the seafood to the Dutch oven. When the milk starts simmering, add the roux back in a tablespoon at a time. Stir and watch as it thickens. It will thicken more with the cheese, so be cautious. You probably won't need all of the roux, and any remainder can be stored in a resealable baggie in the fridge.

Add the cheese, and keep stirring the pot.

When the cheese is melted, garnish the top with parsley and serve it with the bread.

CHAPTER 13
COOKING WITHOUT A RECIPE

I'VE RAMBLED on and on at my blog about food and cooking as "art." By its very nature, art is difficult to define. One man's art is another man's paint spill. Art, in my mind, is basically a vehicle for personal exploration and expression. So in order for an activity to qualify as art, it has to come from somewhere inside me and teach me something about myself, and then it has to help me share that discovery with others.

I think I've only achieved that level a few times in my culinary life. Frankly, I've only done it a few times in song and even fewer in my efforts at visual art. But nonetheless, it is a challenge for me. That's one reason I keep trying.

One thing is for certain: it's difficult to discover something about yourself, and even more so to express that self-awareness, when you're cooking someone else's recipes. The irony of saying that in the context of a cookbook is not escaping me, either.

One of my best friends, Andy Johnson (at backporchgourmet.com), is a big advocate of cooking without recipes and making your own way in the kitchen. In his blog, he summarized it in five rules. With his permission, I've included them here, with my own thoughts.

RULE #1: AT FIRST, MODIFY EXISTING RECIPES.
This is a great way to get started. Take something that's proven to work and tweak it a bit. Add a few more spices or an ingredient that you think will work. Swap out some ingredients. You're not looking for something that's "a good substitute" or even trying to make it "better." You're just trying to make it different.

RULE #2: DO YOUR HOMEWORK. IF YOU WANT TO CREATE SOMETHING ITALIAN, RESEARCH ITALIAN COOKING.
He goes on to say that it's good to recognize the core ingredients in a cuisine. What are the spices and flavors that make a style? If you know these things, you can work better within good parameters.

RULE #3: COMBINE TWO TASTES. THIS IS WHERE FOODS LIKE BARBECUE CHICKEN PIZZA COME FROM.

Then you can start breaking those rules and boundaries, and create "fusion" dishes. These will turn things around and make people's taste buds perk up. "I didn't think you could do those together!"

RULE #4: THROW AWAY YOUR MEASURING CUPS. ESTIMATING YOUR INGREDIENTS AND "WINGING IT" ARE THE FIRST STEPS IN BECOMING A RECIPELESS COOK.

I don't really advocate chucking your tools. Still, I think it's a good idea to be flexible in your amounts. A dash of this, a spritz of that . . . just like the song says. Sometimes that will be to experiment, and other times it will be to your own taste. I never think the recipes call for enough lemon juice or enough garlic.

RULE #5: GRAB A FEW INGREDIENTS AND JUST GO CRAZY.

This is his best idea yet, and the basis for many of our challenge dishes, that I'll be talking about below. Find three core ingredients, even as mismatched as they might seem, and try to make something out of them. There'll be more on this later.

When I read what Andy had written, I got really excited, and I posted some thoughts of my own on Mark's Black Pot:

LEARN FROM OTHERS FIRST

First of all, it's good, as you're learning, to follow the instructions and do the recipes. Being the rebel that I am, I took off on my own way too soon. I do that in life, but that's especially true in the world of Dutch oven cooking. If I had stuck to cooking other people's recipes for a little longer, I would have learned a lot more a lot quicker. It might not have been as much fun, though . . .

Second, watch the right cooking shows. Find shows that actually teach you techniques and skills, not just celebs that throw a few ingredients together. Find shows that teach you why these flavors work together and why you need to hold the knife this way.

And don't waste your time watching competitive cooking. "Chopped" and "The Iron Chef" and other challenge shows are edited for the drama of the competition, not for learning new skills and getting cool ideas.

My favorites are PBS's "America's Test Kitchen" and the Food Network's "Good Eats." Alton Brown is like the Bill Nye of cooking. He's teaching you about the science and art of cooking while being fun to watch. Those two are on permanent record on my TiVo!

START TWEAKING

Third, learn to create hybrid recipes. When you want to cook a particular dish, look on allrecipes.com or recipezaar.com or in your old family cookbooks, and check out several differing recipes for the same dish. Not only will you learn the different approaches, but you'll also pull one idea from one and other ideas from another. In the end, you'll have your own version of a popular dish. My pumpkin pie recipe is a good example of this approach.

RESEARCH HELPS

And fourth, while I'm talking about recipe websites, another thing I like about allrecipes.com is their ingredient search function. Sometimes, I'm looking in my pantry and my fridge, wondering what to cook in my black pots that week. I'll pull up a few ingredients and think, "Can I make something with these?" I'll jump to their ingredient search function and type in those ingredients. It pulls up a bunch of recipes using those ingredients. I read through them and hybrid them and come up with something. This is the process I used, for example, to cook my Dutch Oven Apple Chicken Curry.

Another way to approach this is with culinary reference books, like *Culinary Artistry*. This book is largely a list of ingredients, arranged alphabetically, and following each one is a list of other ingredients and spices that go well with it. Pick what you like, use reasonable amounts, and you've got a whole new dish! I used this approach when I cooked up a salmon and potatoes mix.

NO FEAR!

Finally, be willing to experiment, and be willing to fail. Even as recently as last week, I made a pasta sauce for my parents (in the kitchen, not in the Dutch ovens) that didn't turn out as well as I'd hoped. Learn from your mistakes. Cooking is actually very forgiving. Many things I've cooked that I've considered to be flops are actually edible, even tasty. They weren't quite as amazing as I'd wanted, but they were still good. I've only cooked a few things that I've had to throw away and pronounce inedible.

SHARE AND SHARE ALIKE

Oh! One other thing! When you do create something new, share it! Post it to a recipe site or make your own blog. Don't keep it to yourself. And share more than the recipe. Tell us what you learned and how you did it.

Let us share in your art!

What follows are stories, dishes, and recipes that originated, well, without recipes!

THE DUTCH OVEN CHALLENGES

So, even though Andy and I have been friends for a long time, this whole business started when he issued me a challenge by email one day. I include it here, with his permission:

Mark,

I am throwing down the cast iron gauntlet. I hearby challenge ye to a cast-iron duel. If ye choose to accept the challenge, here are the terms:

1. I will choose 3 ingredients:

   a. Meat

   b. Spice

   c. Fruit or Vegetable or Starch

2. Ye must cook a one-pot Dutch oven dish with the 3 ingredients. Ye may add any additional ingredients so long as they do not nullify these terms. (See number 3.)

   a. The ingredients must be as common and available as possible. I do not expect ye to backpack through the mountains of Nepal for the rare Joo-Joo Truffle or some such.

   b. The ingredients may be up for interpretation. For example, if I say Chicken, ye may use chicken breasts, wings, nuggets, whatever ye wish. If the ingredient specifically states Rib Eye Steak, then there can be no choosing.

      i. Although it states the ingredients may be up for interpretation, meat is meat, so ye may not substitute stock for meat or eggs for meat, although these items could be added. I will, however, consider tofu a meat only because the readers of ye blog may be vegetarian.

      ii. No matter who you talk to, ketchup is not a vegetable.

3. It must be delicious.

4. Ye shall hearby document the entire process, including experiences at the grocery store, prepping the dish, cooking the dish, and most importantly, eating the dish.

5. The recipe shall be original in the whole, and the recipe shall be posted for all to see. (See documentation of step 4.)

6. Ye shall post the experience on the interwebs for all to see and enjoy.

So, do ye accept the challenge? If so, I would expect to see a counter challenge with a list of my ingredients.

If ye be of valor, here are your ingredients. Choose your weapons wisely.

1. Meat—Pork

2. Spice—Curry

3. Fruit/Veg/Starch—Orange

Well, I'm not one to turn down a challenge. Especially from a knight so brave and skilled as Sir Andrew. I quickly responded with this missive:

Andy,

Sorry, I'm lagging way behind. This is a *great* idea. Your challenge ingredients look fun too. It might be as much as a week or two before I get to cooking it, though. Is that okay?

Here are your ingredients:

a. Meat: Fish

b. Spice: Dill

c. Fruit or Vegetable or Starch: Potatoes

The only downside here is that we really should get together and cook these challenge meals, then sample each other's dishes. I just don't know when we could do this.

Mark

Well, we discussed (via electronic carrier pigeon) the possibilities of staging this fated duel face-to-face but soon realized it was a futile effort. We must cook, each man in his own fair land, and the fame of our heated cast-iron battle will needs be shared far and wide in song and legend.

It has been brought!

The whole idea of the challenge wasn't to see who's the best. We really couldn't taste each other's dishes, and there were no judges. The idea was just to push us out of our comfort zones a bit and see what we each can do. And to have a little fun in the process. I tried a little trash talk, but really, I'm not too good at that.

When I went to make my dish, I was really feeling out of the zone. It was strange. Since the original challenge stated that the recipe needed to be "wholly original," I didn't even go online for ideas. I just mulled over ideas in my head and got some great suggestions from my wife.

Here's my result:

ORANGE CURRIED PORK CHOPS

TOOLS
12-inch Dutch oven
15 coals below, 20 coals above

INGREDIENTS
4 cloves garlic, minced
2 medium onions, chopped
5–6 green onions, chopped
4–5 stalks celery, chopped
¼ cup parsley, chopped
1 (13.5-oz.) can coconut milk
1½ cups water
1½ cups rice
salt
pepper

pork chops
kosher salt
curry powder

1 (12-oz.) jar orange marmalade
zest of 1 orange
juice of 1 orange
cinnamon

I STARTED out by chopping up and mincing all of the veggie ingredients in the first set. I mixed all of the first set in the Dutch oven. Pretty easy, so far.

In the next set of ingredients, I had to make some choices. I wasn't sure whether or not I wanted to put the curry directly on the meat, or include it in the glaze. In the end, I decided to put it on the meat. I rubbed the meat, both sides, with kosher salt and curry powder. Then I layered the pork chops over the veggies, rice, and liquid. I had 8 or 9 chops, so I had to overlap them in a circle.

Finally, I mixed the marmalade, zest, juice, and cinnamon into a glop and spooned it onto the meat.

I put that out on the coals. It cooked for a little over an hour. I served it up with a twist of orange and sprinkled with minced mint leaves.

In the end, it was a really interesting flavor. The rice, and even the meat, had a rich creaminess that I'm sure came from the coconut milk. The spices gave it an interesting flavor, one that I'd not tasted before, so it was neat to have something almost completely new.

Here is Andy's response to the challenge, included, again, with his permission:

DUTCH OVEN DUEL:
CREAMED DILL BASA FILLETS WITH POTATO

By Andy Johnson, of backporchgourmet.com

Tonight we came home from church and immediately started working on the Dutch oven duel. I was given fish, dill, and potato. This is what I came up with for the challenge.

I was busy cooking a pig yesterday, so I couldn't go to the store myself. Instead I sent my awesome wife to do the shopping for me. She called me during a very dangerous full contact game of "do you know your neighbor" with the young men and young women of our congregation. She wanted to know what kind of fish fillet to get. I had put flounder, because we saw some frozen flounder at the store, but she had gone to a different store, and they didn't have flounder. I said "Just get the cheapest fillet you can find."

Dangerous words, right? One might think so, but she came home with some basa. I thought they had just keyed in a misspelling when they labeled it, and it was bass. Turns out basa is a catfish that swims in Vietnam and Thailand. You learn something new every day, right? Basa is a very flavorful cut but does not have the fishy taste that turns most people off.

TOOLS
12-inch Dutch oven
15 coals below, 18 coals above

INGREDIENTS
5–6 basa or other fish fillets
dill
salt
pepper
olive oil
balsamic vinegar*
6 Tbsp. butter
1 Tbsp. chopped garlic
3/8 cup flour
1 pint heavy cream
1 cup milk
1 lb. white hard artisan cheese (I used asiago)
5 large potatoes

RUB THE fish fillets with dill, salt, and pepper. Braise the fish in a generous amount of oil. *Spill some balsamic vinegar in the pot by mistake, because it looks exactly like the olive oil bottle.

Sear both sides, then remove and set aside.

Add butter and melt. Add garlic and flour, combining to a blond roux. (A blond roux is golden in color and does not cook much of the flour gluten.)

Remove roux and add cream, half the milk, and generous shakes of dill, salt, and pepper. Add spoonfuls of the roux until the cream sauce thickens. I ended up using it all, and it turned out perfect. When the sauce thickens, grate in about half the cheese, stirring often. Add the potatoes and stir with the cream sauce. Add the fish on the top and grate some cheese on top. Replace the lid and cook for 45 minutes to 1 hour. Serve with bread and steamed vegetables.

My parents gave the dish rave reviews, and my wife, who hates fish, said it was really tasty! Take *that*, Mark!

A SECOND DUTCH OVEN CHALLENGE

Well, one good challenge deserves another, right? I had so much fun being knocked out of my comfort zone, and having it all come out so deliciously, that I was eager to do it again. This time, however, I threw down the offer, and I chose the rules. Most of them were the same, but I changed them up a little bit. I also opened it up to other Dutch oven cooks on the Web, but I wasn't aware if anyone else actually participated.

Here were my rules:

It doesn't have to be a one-pot dish. As long as all of the ingredients end up on the same plate, I don't care how simple or complex the process is.

Once again, the players can add any other ingredients they choose, but the final dish must include all three preset ingredients.

The recipe must be your own original creation. Search the Web and cookbooks for inspiration, but do your own thang.

Rather than require Andy, or anyone else, to come back with a challenge for me, I'm going to also require the same three ingredients for anyone participating.

So here are the new challenge ingredients:

Meat: Beef (any cut or form of it you want)

Veggie/Fruit: Leek, scallion, green onion, and so on

Spice/Flavoring: Cinnamon

Of course, I also undertook the challenge. The process confused me, and in many ways, until I actually did it, I wasn't sure what I was going to do. In my mind, I was going to make the beef and the onions and then do a dairy-based sauce with nutmeg and cinnamon. My main confusion was in how to handle the roux for the sauce. In the end, the process I chose worked, but I might do it differently if I ever do this one again.

I also really struggled to come up with a name for the dish. I asked my blog readers for suggestions, but none were forthcoming. So, it remains . . .

THAT ONE DISH THAT MARK MADE FOR THE DUTCH OVEN CHALLENGE

TOOLS
12-inch Dutch oven
a lot of coals below (for the first steps)
10 coals below, 16 coals above (for the final steps)

INGREDIENTS
2–3 Tbsp. oil
2–3 Tbsp. flour

2–3 cloves garlic
1 medium onion, diced
3 scallions or green onions, chopped
salt

1 lb. ground beef
pepper

2 large potatoes, quartered and sliced
1 sweet pepper, diced

about 2 cups milk
nutmeg
cinnamon
more flour, if necessary, to thicken

I STARTED out by making the roux out of equal parts oil and flour in the open Dutch oven, on bottom heat only. For some reason, my coals were very slow lighting that day, so it took quite a while to make even the blondest of a blond roux. It was also pretty runny.

Once that had cooked a bit, and browned just a little, I added the second set of ingredients, to sauté. I wasn't sure how well it would sauté with the roux still in the pot, but Alton did it once, and it seemed to work, so I guess it was okay. This was a large part of my aforementioned confusion.

Once the onions were translucent, I added the ground beef with the pepper and let that brown.

When the beef was pretty much cooked through and all stirred up, I added the potatoes and sweet peppers. At this point, I covered the Dutch oven and set up the coals for baking/roasting, with top and bottom heat, as listed above. I let the potatoes cook a bit, stirring things up occasionally.

When I could see that the potatoes were starting to cook but not done (maybe just a bit firmer than "al dente"), I poured in the milk. I didn't measure it but rather just guesstimated. I poured it in until it came up to "halfway" covering the meat and potatoes. In other words, there was enough milk that I could see it rising as I poured, but the level of the milk was nowhere near the top of the food. I stirred in the nutmeg and cinnamon and let that cook and simmer some more, covered, until the potatoes were done.

I added just a little more flour for a bit of thickening, but it didn't need much. In retrospect, I'd probably do more roux at the beginning.

I served it up on two slices of the bread I'd made the day before. The tangy bread and the meat made a magnificent combination. From this book, I would suggest using the recipe for Jodi's Sandwich Bread (p. 190), or even the Irish Soda Bread (p. 192).

The taste was delicious, and my son pronounced it "amazing." Another recipe-less challenge was successful!

Here is Andy's dish:

DUTCH OVEN CINNAMON—GLAZED ROAST

By Andy Johnson of backporchgourmet.com

I was really wary about cooking this. After all, beef and cinnamon? Come on, how could I possibly put those together? Mark did a great combo with ground beef and cinnamon served over potatoes and artisan bread. How could I get good results?

I actually had a self-actualizing moment complete with adrenaline rush and heightened senses. It was really cooking zen at its best. You could call it "Cooking on Ten." It's a feeling I can't describe easily. I can't wait to do it again!

TOOLS
12-inch Dutch oven
350 degrees (8–10 coals below, 12–14 coals above) for 60–90 minutes

INGREDIENTS
green onions
1 beef roast

cinnamon
nutmeg
mesquite barbecue spice rub
leeks
barbecue sauce

I STARTED by picking some green onions growing in my garden and diced them small. I cut slits in the roast and stuffed the onions inside. I rubbed the roast with all the spices above and seared all sides. I chopped the leeks and added them to the Dutch oven. I baked it for 60–90 minutes, until the desired cooking temperature was reached. Mine was mostly well done, with just a little bit of rareness. It was so tender.

Andy said that he served it up with potatoes and a dessert, but to get those recipes, you'll have to hit his blog!

Many thanks to Andy for coming up with the idea of the challenges, and for letting me include the results here.

Here's his suggestion for someone wanting to face this kind of challenge, but not knowing who to engage in the battle. Get one or two ordinary six-sided dice and create a table with four columns. One column will be for meats/proteins, another for spices/flavorings, and a third for fruits/veggies/starches. Down one side, number 1–6, for each pip on the die. Then start filling in the columns with ingredients you have on hand. Don't be afraid to get a little bit extreme or to think a little outside of the normal box. That's what this is for, after all, right?

Here's an example of a Dutch Oven Food Challenge Table:

Die Roll	Meats/Proteins	Spices/ Flavorings	Fruits/Veggies/ Starches
1	Beef	Curry	Apples
2	Pork	Oregano/Basil	Celery
3	Chicken	Chili Powder	Tomato
4	Fish	Citrus	Cucumber
5	Eggs	Mint	Hot Pepper
6	Other Seafood	Cinnamon	Asparagus

Using the table is simple too. Just roll the die three times, once for each food column, and those are your three required ingredients. Then combine those three in a new and unique way, and boom, there's your dish!

This table is just a suggestion. You can make your own. If you wanted more options, you could number from 2 to 12 and roll two dice instead of one. If you do that, keep in mind that the numbers in the middle (6–8) will get more rolls than those at the extreme low or high ends. It's a probability thang.

Here are some more original and spontaneously made recipes.

DUTCH OVEN SALMON AND POTATOES

My friend loaned me a really cool book called *Culinary Artistry*, by Andrew Dornenburg and Karen Page. He said it was basically a textbook that he used when he was first employed as a cook. It's seriously cool. The first part has a lot of articles about the authors' philosophies about the nature of food and art. One author discussed how he grew up around food and art, and how he learned to love to experiment. He talked about how we all grow up wanting to try things, but we keep being told, "Don't play with your food!"

His message was now that "I'm a grown-up, I can play with my food!"

Anyway, a large part of the book is basically a reference book. You can look up any primary ingredient, and it will tell you a list of other ingredients and spices and flavorings that "go with it." Some of them go together so well that they're considered "classic combinations," and those are in bold in the list.

One day, I had some frozen salmon left over from a cook-off, so I decided to try something. Rather than find a salmon recipe that spells out exactly how much of everything to put in, I was going to look at this list of compatible ingredients, see what things I already had in my pantry and fridge, and combine them in amounts that made sense!

So, I looked over the list. A few things jumped out at me from the beginning. Potatoes, onions, even bacon. I thought of one of the early dishes I had made with just those three, adding in chicken and cheese. An idea was taking shape.

So here was my final list:

bacon
onions
mushrooms (fresh)
garlic
potatoes
parsley (fresh, if you've got it)
green onions
lemon (zest and juice)
vinegar
red pepper
black pepper
salt
and, for fun, some commercial salmon seasoning I had
water

I STARTED off with the bacon. I cut about a half a pack of it into some small pieces and put them in a 12-inch Dutch oven over about 20 or so coals. Once they were pretty brown and crisp, I drained off most of the grease and added some sliced and separated onions, the sliced mushrooms, and the garlic. I let the onions cook until they were getting clear and a little brown.

Then I quartered and sliced a few potatoes, really thin. Not potato-chip thin, but thinner than I usually slice them. Why? I dunno. Just trying something different. They went into the Dutch oven. I also added in the parsley, sliced green onions, lemon zest, and lemon juice. Then I added in the salmon. I put all that on top of about 8–9 coals and put about 17 on the top. I was going for the basic baking temperature of about 350 degrees.

Then, as it was cooking, I added the seasonings. I also added a little bit of water to help steam the potatoes.

I figured it would cook about 40 minutes or so. I had to keep adding coals because there was a pretty strong and steady breeze blowing, and it kept stoking up my coals. Also, I ended up going almost an hour before the potatoes were fully cooked. I stirred it occasionally to distribute the seasonings. That broke up the salmon too.

For those of you who understand Utah Mormon culture, my wife is the Relief Society compassionate service director for the ward. What that means is that if someone's family has a crisis, she gets to step up and coordinate some help. Sometimes that means cooking some meals while the wife is recovering from an illness, or watching the kids while the mom and dad are at the hospital with another child. It's a cool calling for Jodi, because, frankly, that's the kind of stuff she does even when it's not her gig.

Well, I got to help out today. Part of the reason I cooked was to make enough not only for my family, but also for a family down the street that had just had a miscarriage. We've been there, and it's not fun, believe me. So I got to use my Dutch ovening to help lighten someone else's load.

And where was Jodi during all this? Well, like I said, that's the kind of person she is. She spent the afternoon and evening with another good friend up at the hospital. My wife is amazing.

SEAFOOD CHOWDER

About a year or so ago, I decided I wanted to make seafood chowder. It would have been clam chowder, but we were out of those little cans of clams, and instead we had the little cans of crab and shrimp (about the size of tuna cans, you know— same stuff).

What made it interesting was that I made it without a recipe, with only my brains as my guide. It was exciting to fly without a net, so to speak, and to have it turn out so well.

I used the roux base that my brother-in-law had shown me, and I just treated it a little bit differently, since I wasn't making a cheese sauce.

Anyway, since I didn't have a recipe, I'm just going to talk you through it.

The first thing I did, after lighting up some coals, was get out one of my smaller Dutch ovens and get it on top of about 15 coals or so, so it was getting good and hot. Into that, I put half of a 1-pound package of bacon, cut and separated into little squares. That started cooking.

Once that was going, I got out my 12-inch Dutch oven, which was the one that I was going to do the actual chowder in, and got it on some coals, probably close to 20. I had diced up some onions and minced up some garlic (a couple of cloves), and I got that browning in the 12-inch Dutch oven. At this point, there were no lids on and, obviously, no coals on top.

While that was cooking, I was in the kitchen, quartering and slicing potatoes and slicing some celery. I did about four potatoes, and three or four stalks of celery.

Pretty soon, the bacon was nice and crisp, and the onions were starting to brown. It was a pretty cheap grade of bacon, so there was lots of grease left in the smaller Dutch oven. I pulled the bacon out and put it in with the onions, leaving the drippings. To that, I added some flour. You don't want to add it too quickly, because you could easily add too much. I added until it was a little runnier than cookie dough. I just let it cook, stirring it frequently.

I wanted to see what happened as you cook a roux longer and longer, so I let it go for a while. It gradually got more and more brown. Finally, I saw that it was getting nice and tanned, so I pulled that Dutch oven off the coals.

In the meantime, the onions, garlic, and bacon were still browning nicely in the other Dutch oven. I added a pint carton of cream and about half that much milk, maybe less. To help it boil, I put the lid on. All along this process, I was replenishing my coals as needed from the side fire.

Once it was boiling, I added the potatoes, the celery, and 3 little cans of seafood, with their liquid, to enhance the flavor. Once it was boiling again, I added some of the roux, about a tablespoon at a time, stirring vigorously to break it up in the soup. I watched carefully after each tablespoonful of roux for a minute to check the thickness before adding more. If it goes too thick, I guess you can always just add more milk, but I don't want to catch myself adding and adding to catch up with myself over and over again.

Pretty soon, it was nice and thick but still more of a soup than a sauce. You can make it how you like it.

At that point, I added some parsley, some salt and pepper (all to taste), and also some lemon juice. Then I pulled some of the coals out from under it so it would go from boil to simmer, and put the lid back on.

I checked it about every 15 minutes, just to check the taste and the doneness of the potatoes. It didn't take long, maybe 45 minutes, to be done.

CHICKEN AND APPLE CURRY-OSITY

I think I've found a new favorite recipe website. This week, I had this funny idea of taking some chicken and some apples we had and doing something with them together. It just seemed odd enough to be fun.

But, I had no recipe, so I thought I'd look one up. I'd heard good things about allrecipes.com, so I went there and tried their ingredient search function. I put in "chicken" and "apple" and came up with a whole bunch of recipes. It was a lot of fun to sort through them all.

In the end, what I did was a hybrid of two of the more interesting ones that had other available ingredients.

I'm not sure what to call it, though. Is it a curry? Is it a casserole? I dunno. In the end, I named it the "curry-osity"

TOOLS

12-inch Dutch oven
total of about 30 coals, because of the weather (probably 22–24 in the summer)

INGREDIENTS

oil

1 medium onion, chopped or diced
4–5 cloves garlic, minced
2 stalks celery, chopped
2 lbs. chicken breast, cubed

1 medium to large apple, thinly sliced
2 cups chicken broth
1 cup apple juice concentrate (or about half a can)
1 Tbsp. curry powder
1 tsp. nutmeg
salt and pepper to taste
¼ cup milk
1 cup rice

I STARTED with a little oil on the bottom of the Dutch oven and heated it up over a bunch of coals ("a bunch" is an accurate scientific unit of measurement, larger than "a few" but smaller than "a pile"). I let that heat a bit so I could start sautéing. And that's what I did next, with the first ingredient set after the oil. Actually, I added the chicken in last, after the onions and garlic had had a chance to cook some.

Once everything was getting nicely browned, I just started adding in all of the other ingredients. Because the chicken broth was put in as a frozen block, I let it melt before I added the rice. The stock, by the way, was homemade from our Thanksgiving turkey leftovers.

Also, once the main set of ingredients was in the Dutch oven, I set an even number of coals on the top and bottom. It ended up being about a total of 30 coals, 'cause it was seriously cold out. Outdoor cooking in the winter is odd that way, ya know? I just cooked it until it tasted good and the rice was done.

Anyway, my family loved it, and my son had seconds. That's a good confirmation.

ACKNOWLEDGMENTS

THANKS MILLIONS TO:

MY DEAR WIFE, JODI—I've often heard her say that the first Dutch oven she bought me was the best investment she ever made. It did mean she got her Sunday dinners cooked for her for the next few years. On the other hand, it also meant she's had to try a few flopped meals, and put up with a stressed and frustrated wannabe chef.

BRENDON AND JACOB—My sons, my sous-chefs, and my tasting and testing crew. I'm proud of the things they've learned and the ways they're growing into chefs and young men in their own right.

RUTH AND STEVEN HOLLANDER—My sister and her husband, both better chefs than I will ever be. They are my teachers and advisers. When I want to try something new, I know who I can go to to tell me how to do it best.

LOUISE AND UWE HANSEN—Many thanks to Mom for teaching me to be willing to try new foods and for showing me the basics of cooking. It didn't catch on until much later in life, but I realized how much I'd learned from her, anyway. Dad inspired me in his own way, by his deep appreciation for the things Mom cooked. And thanks, Dad, for the knaeckebrot and the braunschweiger!

JOHN NEWMAN—As I mentioned at the beginning, if it wasn't for John and mormonfoodie.com, I might well have never started Mark's Black Pot. I've learned a lot from him, either by direct instruction or by inspiration. He's also an incredible musician and composer. Through all the bumps over the years, he's remained one of my best friends.

ANDY JOHNSON—Dutch oven aficionado, blogger, gamer, and songwriter. I would have suspected Andy and I were separated at birth if we'd not been born so many years apart. Thank you for the challenges that made me cook on my own.

RANES CARTER—I don't remember how I met Ranes. I do remember him welcoming me, a rank beginner, to share his booth at the IDOS spring convention's Taste of Dutch cooking demo. What a guy, and somehow, through him, I've met a lot more wonderful Dutch oven friends, through the IDOS organization. Many thanks to him and to Ted, Omar, Diane, Colleen, Dave, and many, many others.

SHERSTA GATICA—As of this writing, I've never met Shersta face-to-face, but I hope to soon. I'm very grateful to her that she found marksblackpot.com and saw enough potential there to contact me and present me to her team at Cedar Fort publishing. She's been a great help along the way.

RESOURCES

WONDERFUL DUTCH OVEN AND OTHER COOKING RESOURCES

DUTCH OVEN BLOGS AND INFORMATION WEBSITES

1. Dutch Oven Madness (dutchovenmadness.blogspot.com)
   Toni sets out to cook dinner for her family, outdoors, in her Dutch ovens, every night for a year. Then she keeps going.

2. International Dutch Oven Society (idos.org)
   The premiere society for Dutch oven cooks of all skill levels. Join the forums, check the schedules for gatherings and cook-offs.

3. Byron's Dutch Oven Cooking Page (papadutch.home.comcast.net)
   One of the oldest and most respected sources on the Net for Dutch oven info and recipes.

4. Back Porch Gourmet (backporchgourmet.com)
   Andy's great site about cooking outdoors. "The outdoors starts at your back porch!"

5. Dutch Oven Dude (dutchovendude.com)

6. My Dutch Oven (mydutchoven.com)

DUTCH OVEN MANUFACTURERS

1. Camp Chef (campchef.com)
   Makers and purveyors of all kinds of outdoor cooking supplies, not just great Dutch ovens.

2. Lodge (lodgemfg.com)
   Makers of the first and favorite oven of my collection.

3. Maca (macaovens.com)
   Deep Dutch ovens, some oval for turkeys and larger meats.

GENERAL COOKING INFO

1. Confessions of a Mormon Foodie (mormonfoodie.com)
   John Newman's incredible and inspiring food blog.

2. cooking.com

3. allrecipes.com

4. recipezaar.com

5. sodabread.info

6. chef2chef.net/learn-to-cook/
   A wonderful online cooking class

INDEX

C

D

E

F

G

ABOUT THE AUTHOR

MARK STARTED cooking in his Dutch ovens in 2006, when his wife surprised him with one as a Father's Day present. His first cooking attempt was pizza, and the family instantly declared it a success! He began a tradition of cooking the family's Sunday dinners in his Dutch ovens.

In April of the following year, he thought he should start sharing what he learned and established the Mark's Black Pot blog. Years and hundreds of recipes later, it's still one of the most widely read Dutch oven blogs on the Net.

Mark lives in Eagle Mountain, Utah, with his wife, Jodi, and two boys, who are also budding chefs.